farkhondeh Shahroudi

liebe,liebst,liebt,lieben,liebt,lie ben,liebte,liebtest,
liebte,liebten,liebtet, liebten nich,liebtet
Transitiv
liebe,schaukelnde korpus eine textstube auf maibachufer:
begeisterteschatten
liebten,falle in eine sprachlücke hinein,da liegst du
liebe,erwische mich selbst in millionen lichtjahren
entfernt von deiner wange
liebtest,ich erkenne dich
liebtet,du bist ein aus der rache in kindheitshinein hustende
schwan,du kennst ölöfen markearj nicht
liebten,einbeinige humpelnde taube bistdu,du roboter
nachtigall,mischung einer notfalldienst warnsignal,
verblästes vogelgezwischer bist du
liebst,verdächtige ich dich als briefwurm
lieben,auf meine loggia,du magst in eine muschel sumsen
liebten,wenn luftmoleküle beginnen unsere körper zu
stechen
liebt,du vertreibst fliegen in linden sommertagen
nach aachen
liebten,dorn eine rose ist gegen lauschangriff
liebling nimm mich geiseln,du schwaches
unregelmessiges verb

عاشقم ، عاشقی ، عاشقست ، عاشقیم ، عاشقید ، عاشقند

عاشق بودم ، عاشق بودی ، عاشق بود ، عاشق بودیم ، عاشق بودید

عاشق بودند ، عاشق نیستی

فعل ناگذرا

عاشقم ، کالبد آگورنگ چربی ، [illegible] کانال مایباخ اوغار ، غوطه ور

دریا به ، تا به اشباح ، مشتاق سایه‌ها

عاشق بودیم ، سقوط در گردی حرف ع ، تو آنجا چمبانمه زدی

عاشقم ، پیچ خودم را می‌گیرم ، در میلیون‌ها سال نوری ، و دراز کرده‌ی ، تو

عاشق بودی ، تو را به خانه‌ام آورم

عاشق بودید ، تو قوهست و من در یک هست ، سرمه می‌کنی ، جایی نقطه‌ای را نمی‌شناسی

عاشق بودند ، تو کبوتر یک پای لنگانی ، تو رقص ربات ، نک بلبلی ، آوازی پژمرده

تلمیغی از آذر بر آسید اسنس و چهچه‌ی

عاشقی ، مشکلم که حرز نامه‌ای یا کرم نامه‌ای

عاشقیم ، یک ایران و دست داری در گردش نگ صف پیچ پیچ کنی

عاشق بودیم ، موقتی مولکول‌های هوا بی تن مائوزک ی زنده

عاشق است ، تو در روزهای گرم تابستان مسبب وزار مگس‌هایی

عاشق بودیم ، تیغ کل ضد استراق سمع است

عاشق ایم که با بادبان‌های سوراخت مرا به گردکان تکبیری

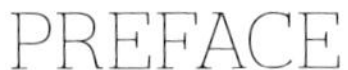

This publication is released on the occasion of Farkhondeh Shahroudi's US debut exhibition, *of weeping trees* (2024), at the Goethe-Institut New York. However, this should not be confused with an exhibition catalogue. Instead, we present a retrospective glance at the pivotal moments and major series in Shahroudi's practice, stretching as far back as her figurative paintings from her time as a student and extending as recently as the 2024 works made during her residency at the International Studio and Curatorial Program (ISCP) in Brooklyn, New York. In this publication, the authors and I dive into Shahroudi's rich practice, privileging the artwork and contextualizing her artmaking within a wider concept of worldbuilding.

Nevertheless, any publication on Shahroudi would be remiss not to mention her biography as an artist forcibly displaced from her homeland and living in an adopted country. Born and raised to a politically active family in Iran, Shahroudi organized and participated in actions during and after the 1979 Revolution, alongside her comrades in the communist Tudeh Party, youth and women's organizations, and other leftist causes. She remained in Iran for about a decade after the Revolution, however it became apparent that a continued life in the newly founded Islamic Republic was untenable, to say the least. She fled to Paris, and eventually settled in Dortmund, Germany in 1990, where she lived and continued her arts education before relocating to Berlin permanently in 2001. While Shahroudi's background indeed sheds light and context on her work, it would be a devastating mistake to essentialize and reduce her artistic practice exclusively through the lens of her immigration. These days, Shahroudi is often heralded as an "artist in exile"—a label which she neither fully rejects, nor fully embraces. ("It is factual, but it is not the whole story," as she relayed to me).

With this in mind, the invited authors, Jordan Amirkhani, and Billy Fowo, and I approach Shahroudi's work from different angles. My contribution thinks through Shahroudi's splintering of herself as a catalyst for her creative production. Psychoanalytically driven, the fracturing of the image of self allows Shahroudi to share parts of her psyche with her audience while also maintaining a private interiority.

Billy Fowo considers Shahroudi's language as both private and public—as a bridge between cultures in service of co-creating a world alongside those with whom she is in community. Fowo provides us with personal anecdotes and embodied knowledge, intertwined with vignettes into Shahroudi's particular use of language and poetry.

Concluding the book, Jordan Amirkhani takes a post-colonial and historical perspective to situate Shahroudi's work in relation to the concepts of garden and utopia in Persian culture. The reception of textiles within the art historical canon informs how Amirkhani thinks and writes about Shahroudi's engagement with the traditional Persian carpet as a medium.

Cumulatively, our different perspectives contribute to a growing body of writing on Shahroudi's work that begins to unpack some of the internal tensions found within her oeuvre and shifts the focus away from a politics of identity and nationhood towards one of exploration, interpersonal relationships, and psychological investigations.

— Zachary B. Feldman

ZACHARY B. FELDMAN
Hair, Mouth, Hands, and Feet: Totems of Access

When encountering the work of Farkhondeh Shahroudi, one cannot help but feel close to the mind of the artist. The viewer is struck with a feeling of uncanniness among the surreal forms and unconventional media that seem familiar but are not immediately recognizable. Shahroudi's works do not labor to explain themselves, yet they compose a coherent, albeit mysterious, aura that compels deeper looking. This is compounded further by the immersive experience that Shahroudi offers— it seems impossible to confront a lonesome work as the art itself demands a certain maximal aesthetic, whether viewed in the gallery or in her studio. Working with a vast breadth of media including painting, sculpture, artist books, textiles, video, photography, performance, and more, Shahroudi's work reads at once melancholic and joyful, political and innocent, humanoid and animal-istic. As I demonstrate, along with the other authors in this publication, tension is a central concept to Shahroudi's oeuvre. It pervades every facet of Shahroudi's works and engenders a body of uneasy pieces that challenge the viewer's impulse to understand. Prominent among these tensions is a fracturing of the physical and metaphori-cal body into pieces, some of which are offered gently to the public, while others are reserved and directed inwards to the artist's drive to explore her own psyche.

In one of my many conversations with the artist as we were creating the exhibition *Farkhondeh Shahroudi: of weeping trees* at the Goethe-Institut New York, Shahroudi recounted an important moment for herself as an artist. A feeling shared by many displaced people —particularly forcibly displaced people—Shahroudi struggled with questions of national and social belong-ing in Germany and eventually sought the care of a psychoanalyst. During her treatment, she came to have an epiphany that liberated her from the pull between her bequeathed Persian-ness and her newly acquired German-ness: "I am an artist," she claimed then and there, relegating the entire question of national belonging to an important, yet secondary tier that serve only the purposes of issuing passports, paying taxes, and the like. Shahroudi's rejection of national identity and the positivist declaration of herself as an artist is still evident in her work, particularly in the performance series with accompanying sculptures entitled *antiflag* (2017–ongoing). The "flags" themselves can be comprised of nearly anything—braided artificial hair, handmade banners with embroidered phrases, and woven bicycle tubes have been employed by Shahroudi for this purpose. The *antiflag* performances are deceptively simple— the flags are waved, sometimes while Shahroudi recites poetry and other times in silence. What is persistent throughout, however, is a refusal to align the personal and the state. Shahroudi's flags are her own, and as such, they undo any notion of mass unity under their banner.

Working with a process-based and intuitive practice, Shahroudi steps into a trance-like state in her artmaking. It is indivisible from her life: When in residence at the International Studio and Curatorial Program (ISCP), she regularly spent 10- to 12-hour days working away in her small Brooklyn studio—a process she describes, perhaps counterintuitively, as orienting herself to a new locale. Her works appear to be a biproduct of her psychology and state-of-being, and therefore center the things that are most important to her: kinship, language, and self-inquiry.[1] Shahroudi's works are political insofar as she is a political subject with political convictions, but they can hardly be accused of didacticism. Where politics are addressed in Shahroudi's works, they are entangled in and inextricable from her subjectivity; that is to say, her works are an extension of herself and her mind, offered up to the public with a polite reservation that preserves a layer of intimacy and privacy the viewer cannot access.

[1] Shahroudi claims that all her works "derive from her unconscious." See Peter Chametzky, *Turks, Jews, and Other Germans in Contemporary Art* (Cambridge, MA: The MIT Press, 2021), 169. This is further evidenced by her use of automatic writing—a writing tradition associated with spirituality and the Surrealists—that is explained in greater detail in Billy Fowo's essay in this publication.

Still, Shahroudi leaves breadcrumbs for us to follow. Fracturing the body—usually her own—she uses hair, mouth, hands, and feet to signify the segments of her subjectivity that interact with the world. One of Shahroudi's earliest videos, *tab* (2005) features a series of clips with no sound: First, the artist brushes her hair with her face turned away from the camera, then uses her hands to rub red paint on to her feet. The video cuts to a closeup from her nose to her chin mouthing soundless words, then shifts again to her hands now sewing green cloth. The final sequences show the artist running a knife's blade between her lips and finally, cutting camouflage patterned fabric with a pair of scissors. The bizarre is interspersed with the quotidian and recalls a muted violence in this puzzling short video. The camera cuts her into discrete elements, though the whole is withheld. We see glimpses of her through the accessible portals: hair, mouth, hands, and feet. The hands and feet interact with exterior objects—the hands rub the feet, spreading red paint over both, and the hands also perform the dialectical activities of cutting and sewing. The mouth,

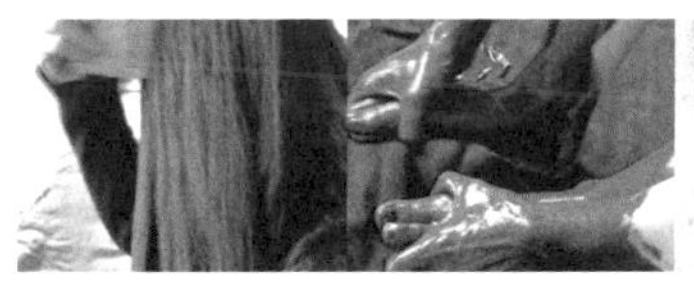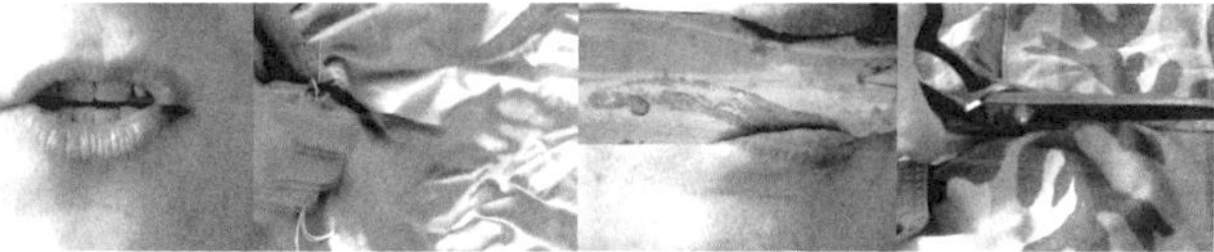

tab (stills), 2005. Courtesy: the artist

however, is silent. Shahroudi's lips form words and even sentences perhaps, although without sound they are rendered mute. Still, *tab* frames Shahroudi herself, face turned away and profiled only in fleeting glimpses, as she pulls a fine-toothed comb through her hair. In this short video and elsewhere in Shahroudi's practice, hair is prominent not only as a subject, but also as a medium.

Hair—that is, artificial hair (or *Kunsthaar*[2] in German)— is ubiquitous in Shahroudi's works. Buying it by the bundle from the *Afroshop*[3] on the ground level of her studio building, she uses the material in numerous ways: braiding it into long ropes, twisting it into thin locks that are woven together, wrapping it around flexible tubing, and more. Using hair as a medium invokes obvious references to the history and policing of women's hair in Iran, where the hijab was banned by the government from 1936 until the 1979 Revolution. After, the law was overturned (along with the Shah), and the concealment of women's hair was made mandatory —a battle which has ignited civil disobedience and brutal oppression of the people by the current Iranian regime in recent years until today. While one could argue that the use of artificial hair in Shahroudi's work is purely logistical, it seems more likely to me an intentional decision (consciously or unconsciously) to evoke the symbolic hair, yet maintain distance from it—a familiar tactic in her practice, and one that conjures internal tension. Real hair, presented in the quantities used by the artist, would perhaps be already overdetermined with unavoidable connotations, particularly within the German context.[4] The use of artificial hair instead connotes the material reality—in both senses of the phrase—of hair and its cultural significance, yet, it is *not* real hair, and as such hollows out a gap for the viewer to fill in.

[2]   The formulation of the word in German is particularly notable, as "Kunst" means "art,"
        but can be added as a prefix to indicate the artificiality of the noun it modifies.
[3]   *Afroshops* refer to stores in Germany that carry food, cosmetic, cultural, and other miscel-
        laneous items for diasporic populations residing in German cities. As the name indi-
        cates, they often cater to African populations, but in large multicultural cities such as Berlin,
        the shops may be inclusive of other populations.
[4]   Heaps of human hair are often used as a symbol of the Holocaust, during which prison-
        ers of the concentration camps were forcibly shaved and their hair was integrated into
        industrial supply chains.

Another example of the evocation and distanciation that reoccurs throughout Shahroudi's oeuvre is the portrayal of mouths that do not speak—although they wish to do so—such as the sequence in *tab*. The analog photographic series, *ausfinger* (from finger, 2003), features Shahroudi with most of her face shrouded, bound, and gagged by cloth. Other photographs in the series feature the knife from *tab*, now pointed at Shahroudi's mons pubis, framed on either side by a red scarf.[5] The recurring use of the knife on the mouth and the groin link the silencing of women with sexual violence, and is one of the few explicit references of violence in Shahroudi's oeuvre—she references, but does not reproduce it. Although the mouth may be prohibited from speaking—under threat of violence, a chilling effect,

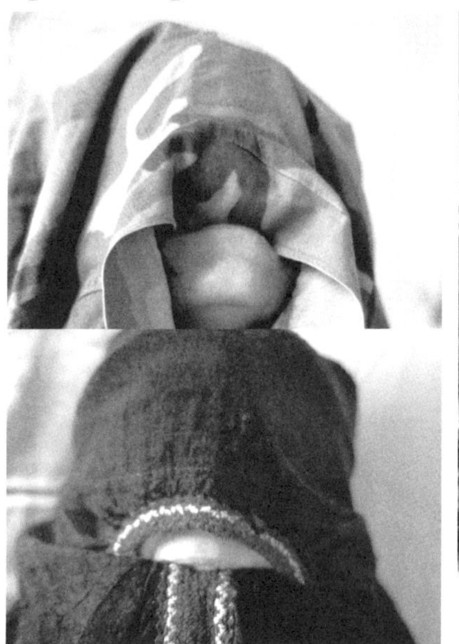
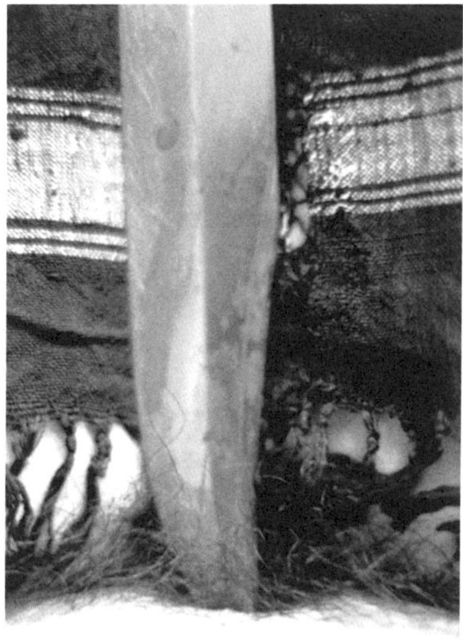

From the series *ausfinger*, 2003. Courtesy: the artist

or otherwise—communication still occurs, but is transferred into a different realm.

[5]   There is another photograph in this series that replaces the knife with a swatch of Persian carpet. In a similarly dated photographic series, *extasy* (2003), the carpet stands in for a bullet, implying a larger equivocation at this time in Shahroudi's work between the Persian carpet and bodily violence. It is notable that Shahroudi always *détourns* the Persian rug in some way or another, never leaving it as it is. Anecdotally, she once explained to me the cold shoulder she sometimes receives from carpet wholesalers once they realize her Leftist politics, since many of the sellers are royalists and maintain a nostalgic loyalty to the Shah. Although I touch on it, a larger reflection of the representation and function of violence in Shahroudi's work is still necessary at a future date.

Hands (and feet, too) persist throughout Shahroudi's practice, often symbolizing the liminal space between the body and its environs. Her series from 2001-05, *wächter* (guards) and *taubstumm* (deaf and dumb, 2003-04)[6] offer a comparative reading through the absence of, and respectively exclusive use of, hands to represent the body and language. *wächter* showcases a series of altered military fatigues in camouflage (likely the same cloth featured in *tab*). Shahroudi intervenes by sewing the open seams around the arms, legs, and neck shut, often adding or removing limbs in the process. In doing so, she transforms the garment into a closed system that embodies its own agency separate from the human wearer; it can no longer be worn like clothing and instead resembles a puppet-like form. Alternatively, *taubstumm* displays the opposite ethos. Comprised of hand-embroidered and sewn gloves, each one attaches to another in a petrified gesture, leaving

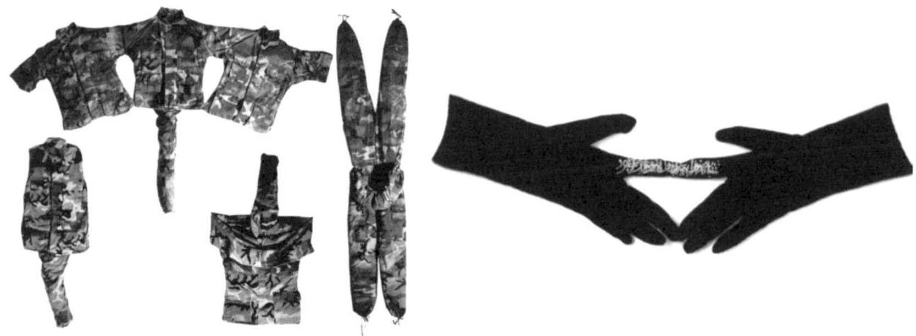

From the series *wächter*, 2001-05. Courtesy: the artist
From the series *taubstumm*, 2003-04. Courtesy: the artist

the structure of the gloves open and still technically able to be worn on the hands. *taubstumm* and *wächter* are counterpart series that, when read together, imply a fundamental closure of the body to the outside world. In this way, the body and the mouth are similar; they are open systems turned closed—modes of "speech" shut down, and shut up. Conventional communication is dislocated and instead expressed through the hands— and is not without precedent. In his 1997 film, *Ausdruck der Hände (The Expression of the Hands)*, Harun Farocki uses fragments of Hollywood and arthouse cinema through the ages to trace how close-ups on hands have operated in the filmic image. The voiceover states:

> The first close-ups in the history of film were of the face; the next featured human hands. Often, hands are supposed to betray something hidden in the expression of the face. For example, the hand might tightly hold onto a glass, while the face appears calm.[7]

This certainly holds true in Shahroudi's work, where hands, typically disembodied, reveal what the body and the mouth cannot. In *taubstumm* the gloves are inscribed with hand-embroidered poems in Farsi that literally gesture towards the metaphoric as Shahroudi's primary form of communication. The hands are the locus of the artist's poetic inscriptions, legible only to those who know Farsi.[8]

[6] Both terms, in German and in English, are pejorative and antiquated descriptions of deaf and hard of hearing people (*gehörlose Menchen*, in German). In this text, I reuse this language to refer exclusively to the titular artworks and recognize the diverse methods of shared communication in the deaf and hard of hearing community.

[7] *Ausdruck Der Hände (The Expression of Hands)*, directed by Harun Farocki, Filmproduktion & WDR, 1997.

[8] This is an important point, because the artist typically exhibits in spaces in Europe where the majority of visitors are unlikely to be Farsi speakers or readers. Therefore, Shahroudi's use of her native language for these poems creates an in-group who have a bit more access to the artist. See Fowo's essay in this publication for more on this topic.

Farsi is a language reliant upon the use of idiomatic phrases and expressions, many of which include common parts of the body to communicate different meanings. Some of these include the head, the eye, the heart, the back, and also the hand (دست, or "dast") and the foot (پا, or "pā"). The latter two words have broad definitions referencing both physical body parts (from the shoulder to the fingertip and from the upper thighs to the toes, respectively) and a multitude of associative meanings.[9] One recent sociological study of 10,000 Persian proverbs referencing "pā" determined the foot to be "conceptualized as being either tantamount to or being in the locality of feelings, thoughts, memories, and personality traits."[10] The authors claim that it "provides a conceptual foundation for speakers of Persian to represent their cognitive, emotional, socio-cultural, and linguistic experiences." In other words, the study situates "pā" as a physical and emotional foundation, and as a pillar of inter- and intrapersonal sociality.

[9]   Persian Language Online (blog), "Persian Expressions with Body Parts 5: دست Dast 'hand' and پا Pā 'Foot,'" November 11, 2022. https://persianlanguageonline.com/persian-expressions-with-body-parts-5-دست-dast-hand-and-پا-pa-foot/.

[10]   Ali Rahimi and Zeynab Karimi, "Conceptualization of 'Foot' Metaphors in Persian and English Idioms/Proverbs: An Intercultural Communication Study," *International Journal of New Trends in Social Sciences* 5, no. 2 (December 31, 2021): 125–35. https://doi.org/10.18844/ijntss.v5i2.5879. Also see Nahid Ahangari, "Conceptualization of *Sar* (Head) in Persian Figurative Expressions," *International Journal of Language and Culture*, November 7, 2023. https://doi.org/10.1075/ijolc.00044.aha.

Shahroudi's film *ou* (2012) prominently features a still image of the artist's foot with a torn sock (the image derives from a 2004 analog photo, *füsskleider* [foot clothing]) overlaid by animated text of the Farsi word او (translated as third person singular pronouns "he/she/it") and a haunting soundtrack, in which the word is repeated in the artist's voice. Given the aforementioned sociological analysis, *ou* gestures towards the relationality between the artist herself and those who are interpel-

18

lated as subjects by the video's call—which is to say, all of us, albeit indirectly. Similarly to how Shahroudi's hands communicate, the feet, too, call out into the world from which the rest of the body, but particularly the mouth, seems to retreat.

One element of Shahroudi's practice that has been considered at length in writings on her work is her conceptualization of all her art, regardless of media, as poetry.[11] The sculptures jump off the page into three-dimensional space, and text is integral to each medium in which she creates. Metaphor is the primary force behind her poetic means of communication. Farsi is often colloquially described as one of the most poetic languages,[12] and while there may be some anecdotal truth to this, the framing too often conflates language and identity, and posits an inherent intentionality to the language itself. Instead, I view metaphor as the ultimate site of tension in Shahroudi's work; between her unquenchable desire to understand herself and communicate that self to her public, and a desire—perhaps motivated by the discrimination, oppression, and surveillance she has faced first-hand—to maintain privacy. Psychoanalysis, in its clinical practice, provides exactly that: The analysand allows the analyst access into her mind and most private memories, drives, and unconscious, yet within the framework of medical privacy and confidentiality.

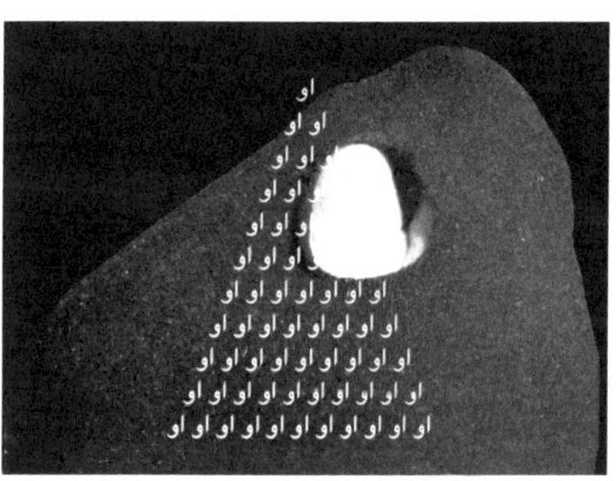

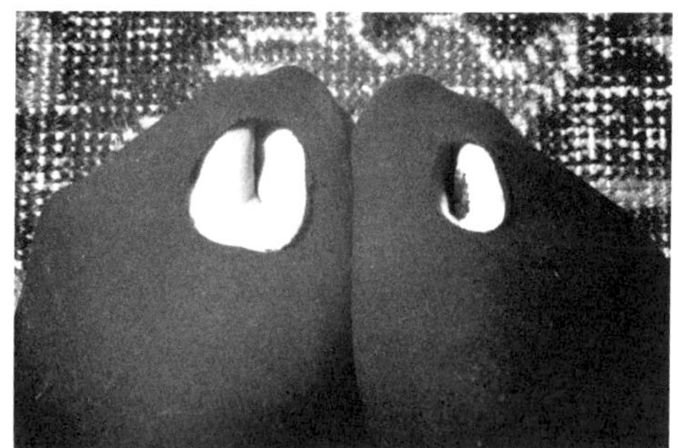

ou (still), 2012. Courtesy: the artist
fusskleider, 2003. Courtesy: the artist

Shahroudi's practice is undergirded by this structure but transposed onto the relationship between artist and viewer. Unlike the analyst, however, the viewer's desire for more access does not arise from a trained perspective, nor is it regulated by laws or professional codes. Shahroudi, staunch in her kinship in relation to her community and individualism in relation to the state, is split between drives to share and retreat. She responds with a public fracturing of self through conscious and unconscious means. Some fragments are given to her viewer as totems of access to herself, while other fragments are safeguarded in order to preserve a psychic interiority. What we make of these fragments, however, is up to us—and we shall handle them with care.

[11]   See Dr. Alma-Elisa Kittner, "blossoming. Farkhondeh Shahroudi's spatial poetry and poetic-political spaces," in *Wir sind die Feder in des Schreibers Hand, wohin wir gehen, ist uns nicht bekannt · Farkhondeh Shahroudi* (Berlin: Staatliche Museen zu Berlin · Preußischer Kulturbesitz, 2023).

[12]   It is interesting, however, that this, too, is often said of the German language.

BILLY FOWO

Speaking In Tongues: A Rumination on Farkhondeh Shahroudi's Plurilingual Worlds in Three Acts

To write about the works of Farkhondeh Shahroudi is to embark on a journey built from words and scripts—a journey characterized by plurilingualism, in which a word in German opens up to one in English, one in English leads to Farsi, and all these various languages co-exist with one another. Writing about Shahroudi's works entails dissecting an artistic practice that spans over several decades and different genres traversing painting, sculpture, bookmaking, and many more. Although her works could be clustered into these different categories, the red thread linking them together is, without any doubt, the poetic touch present in all of her pieces.

ACT 1: FARKHONDEH IS HERE

Every language opens up a different viewpoint to the world.[1]

I first met Farkhondeh Shahroudi in 2021 when I visited her studio. From first sight, I was quite impressed by the meticulous display of each artwork. Her studio, full of completed and in-progress works was, as I later learned, how the artist describes it herself: an "exhibition draft." If the artist studio can be considered as a site of continuous productivity par excellence, in Shahroudi's case it is indeed that, and much more. To quote the artist, "The studio is a reflection of my artistic and creative process, and every day I come in and work on new pieces to be displayed along already existing ones within an exhibition that constantly shifts over time."[2] For Shahroudi, the studio, though not an exhibition hall, is a dialogic space where the addition   23

and/or removal of a piece further expands discourse
and opens up new questions.

[1]   Translated by the author from the French "Chaque langue a une vision du monde partic-
       ulière." Excerpt from Arlette Pacquit, *Monchoachi, La parole sovaj*, 2021.
[2]   From an in-person conversation between the author and the artist. Translated from German
       to English for this text.

In the documentary *Monchoachi, La parole sovaj* (2021),
the Martinican poet Monchoachi describes every language as a potential viewpoint through which the world
can not only be seen, but also inhabited. One of the
most striking aspects upon entering Farkhondeh's studio
is the presence of numerous texts written in black
font, diligently inscribed over the transparent windows
and upon the white walls. Written primarily in German,
the texts invite the visitor into Shahroudi's viewpoints
on the world through languages. In one corner of the
room is written the sentence *farkhondeh is here*—one of
the few visible traces of the artist's use of the English
language. One can justifiably read this daily reminder
as an artist claim to mark her presence, but it can also
be perceived as a welcome notice—a greeting to anyone
entering her studio and, by extension, her world. On an
opposite wall across the studio stand hand-knitted
sculptures, textiles carrying Farsi scripts referring to the
artist's Iranian background, a sewing machine, and left
over fabric on the floor hinting to the artist's affinity
for textiles. Shahroudi's studio is a living space in which
the five senses get triggered. I can vividly remember
the smell of tea herbs brewing upon arrival and the sight
of pistachios served on a plate while we were conversing.
But Shahroudi's presence is one that you feel beyond
her studio. By writing and painting on the glass windows, Shahroudi plays with notions of privacy, interior,
exterior, and belonging. Her studio—located on the top
floor of a building in the Wedding Höfe, a neighborhood

in Berlin where many people with immigrational background live, work, flow in and out for daily groceries—
is one that is buoyant and affords little privacy. It is also
a neighborhood where anyone with a *Migrationshintergrund,*
or migration background, in Berlin feels a sense of
belonging. By inscribing these texts both in German and
Farsi on the windows, Shahroudi not only creates a
bridge with these immediate neighbors (who are, after
all, her first audience), she also inscribes herself within
this group that contributes to pluralizing the neighborhood, and the city of Berlin more largely.

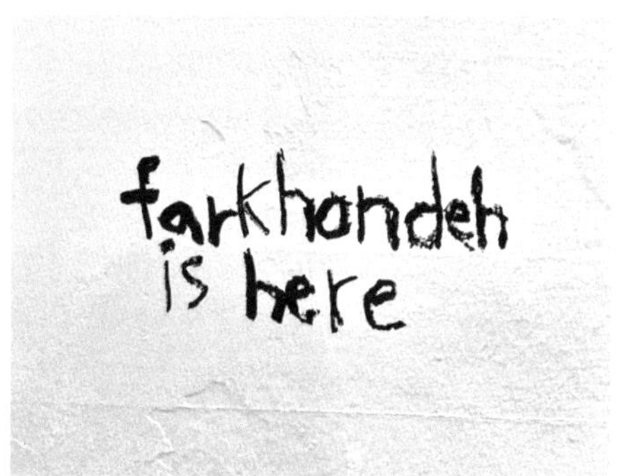

"farkhondeh is here" inscribed on the wall of the artist's studio, Berlin.
Courtesy: Zachary B. Feldman

While in residency at the International Studio and Curatorial Program (ISCP) in Brooklyn,
New York, Shahroudi reinscribes her presence, this time with a temporal conditioner.
Courtesy: Zachary B. Feldman

ACT 2: GLOSSOLALIA

English
is my mother tongue.
A mother tongue is not
not a foreign lan lan lang
language
l/anguish
      anguish
-a foreign anguish.

English is
my father tongue.
A father tongue is
a foreign language,
therefore English is
a foreign language
not a mother tongue.[3]

Shahroudi's story is one that is shared by millions of others who, upon arrival to a foreign country, must learn to integrate into a new and often hostile environment. Although I moved to Germany twenty-five years after Shahroudi did, facing the harsh German bureaucracy and moving pass the linguistic barriers are experiences I, too, share. But how long does it take for one to be considered integrated within the new society? Is it when one, through the difficulty and despite the violence, finally masters the foreign language to the point where it becomes a first language?

[3]   M. NourbeSe Philip, "Discourse on the Logic of Language," in *She Tries Her Tongue, Her Silence Softly Breaks* (1989, Middletown: Wesleyan University Press, 2014), 30-33.

In 2008, Shahroudi began to work on an ongoing series entitled *glossolalie, automatic writing.* In various

religious practices, *glossolalia,* or the act of speaking
in tongues, refers to speaking a language that is foreign
both to the speaker and to the audience. It is believed
that speaking in tongues would require the intercession
of an outer earth force and could only be understood
by God. In *glossolalie, automatic writing,* Shahroudi rein-
vestigates this notion of foreignness and highlights the
painful process of learning and mastering a foreign language to the point where it becomes a mother tongue.
The work consists of paper bound books written and
drawn with her non-dominant left hand in German.
glossolalie, automatic writing hints to Shahroudi's ability
to take in and give back information from and about
her surroundings, while simultaneously processing
them. The procedure of automatic writing has become
integral to Shahroudi's practice over the past decades,
whereby the artist has trained her brain into using her
left hand perfectly just as she would use her right, so
that this act becomes an automatic one. Metaphorically,
the tedious act of training the brain to produce this
automatic writing is analogous to the strain experienced
throughout one's integration into a new society. Getting
to the point where this act becomes automatic—and
by extension one that could be dissociated to a strenu-
ous bodily experience—requires passing through
"foreign anguish" as described by Trinidadian poet
M. NourbeSe Philip in "Discourse on the Logic of Language."
Like Philip's mother and father tongue of English,
Shahroudi, by training herself into using her left hand,
incorporates the pain and pleasure of acquiring the
flow of expression associated with gaining an additional
mother tongue. Through this act, the artist also questions the idea that someone's mother tongue is always
necessarily and inextricably linked to their place of

birth. In acquiring the skills required to speak and write in German, Shahroudi, though born in Tehran, blurs the notion of German-ness, from a linguistic perspective. Alongside *glossolalie, automatic writing*, the series *book in the book* (2001-ongoing) form a larger body representative of Shahroudi's practice around bookmaking. The works recall the Persian tradition of manuscript making and consist of books and scripts on fabric upon which Shahroudi writes in Farsi—her mother tongue—and draws using solely her right hand. Books are something special for Shahroudi, as they played a major part of her childhood. Shahroudi, who grew up in a household with her father owning a bookstore, bathed in the rich tradition of Persian poetry and miniature, the forms and aesthetics of which now reflect in her artist books. The books, some of which contain holes that foreshadow information hidden pages ahead, while others display drawings that span and expand over pages like a flip-book, add a playful tone to Shahroudi's works, circling back to her childhood memories growing up in her father's bookstore.[4]

[4]   Due to her father's activism the bookstore was burned down, and this led to the family subsequently fleeing to Tehran.

Notions of legibility and illegibility are prominent characteristics of plurilingualism in Shahroudi's practice. In her series *book in the book*, Shahroudi writes several layers in Farsi over each other rendering the script illegible. By repeating the action of writing over and over again, Shahroudi creates a new language—one particular to her artistry and a desire for a public private hybridity. These scripts, though illegible from up close, portray a visual language containing sculptural and design elements that, when seen from afar, recall the artist's earliest paintings. This is representative   28

of a larger conceptual framing that Shahroudi imagines,
in which all her work is understood as three-dimensional
poetry—whereby the letters, words, and scripts from
her texts manifest within space as sculptural form. On one
occasion, words painted over bread can be seen displayed on a table, as if referring to a banquet or to the
Last Supper. On another occasion the onomatopoeia
"oh" can be seen floating in space or resting against a
wall as a sculpture, activating our imaginary and invit-
ing the viewer to consider what must have preceded
these anonymous exclamations.[5]

[5]   Angelika Stepken, "Give something of yourself," in *wir sind die feder in des schreibers hand,
       wohin wir gehen, ist uns nicht bekannt – Farkhondeh Shahroudi* (Berlin: Archive Books, 2023), 87.

By using Farsi within the German context, Shahroudi
renders text "illegible" and deliberately refuses to con-
form to the norms of legibility channeled only through
the German language. In rendering Farsi "indecipher-
able" through her palimpsest-like process and a refusal
of German language in German spaces, Shahroudi
reserves the right to be opaque, simultaneously extending an invitation to question what and why something
is foreign, all the while welcoming into her fold those

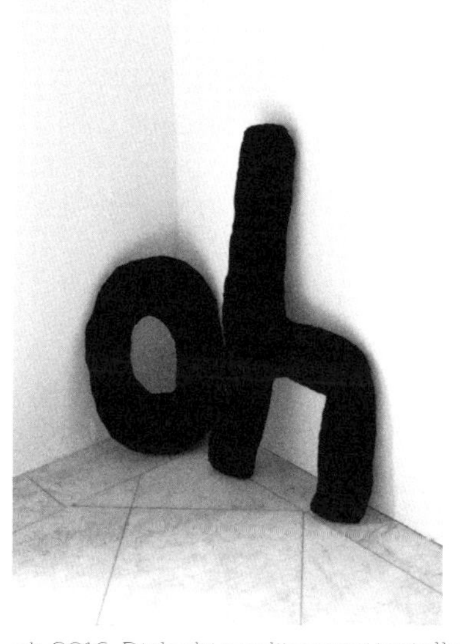

oh, 2016, *Dialoghi mediterranei* installation view at Villa Romana, Florence, 2017. Courtesy: the artist

who are perceived as speaking in tongues within the
German context. Furthermore, these works comment
on that which can be translated and that which is
untranslatable, which we might extrapolate as the tension between public and private. Recalling the earlier
quote by Monchoachi, "Every language opens up a
different viewpoint to the world." Yet, some bodily per-
ceptions and ways of inhabiting the world are simply
untranslatable from one language to the other. Shahroudi
plays with the shared and private languages by exploring the limits of untranslatability not only between Farsi
and German, but between a public, shared Farsi, and
a private, journalistic writing, embroidered like a palimp-
sest and condensing linear writing into a singular point.

ACT 3: A CALL FOR WORLD-MAKING THROUGH POETRY

We often tell our students, the future's in your hands.
But I think the future is actually in your mouth.
You have to articulate the world you want to live in first.[6]

There is a popular saying in French (my mother tongue)
that one needs to "curl their tongue seven times in their
mouth before saying anything."[7] If we take this literally
to mean that one must think thoroughly before speaking, the proverb motions towards the mighty power of
speech to both construct and destruct. In a conversation
with the journalist Krista Tippett, the Vietnamese-
American poet Ocean Vuong spoke to the future of languages as something of which we are all participants;
language only lives insofar as it is used.[8] By referring
to the world as constantly made, and re-made, through   30

oral articulation, Vuong shifts the attention away from the hands as a tool of making unto the mouth.

[6]   Extract from a conversation between Krista Tippett and Ocean Vuong, "A Life Worthy of Our Breath," *On Being*, aired April 30, 2020. Quote by Ocean Vuong.
[7]   Translated from the French "Tourner sa langue sept fois dans sa bouche avant de parler."
[8]   Krista Tippett and Ocean Vuong, "A Life Worthy of Our Breath," *On Being*.

It is precisely this world-making endeavor through linguistic construction that Shahroudi embraces and utilizes in her work. In a conversation with Shahroudi in November 2023, I asked her about the importance of multiple languages in her work.[9] She stated simply, "Sprache ist unzertrennlich von meiner Künstlerischen Arbeit," or "Language is inseparable from my artistic work." By writing, stitching, reading, and performing in different languages (Farsi, German, and English), Shahroudi creates and connects the space between languages: The untranslatable and the unable to be said. As a poet, Shahroudi sends out an invitation to think and breath within the realm of poetry—perhaps one of the few accommodating fields that makes space to rethink, re-articulate, create new words and meanings—to imagine and speak out the worlds we want to live in, before, potentially, building them with our hands.

[9]   The conversation occurred on November 12, 2023, during the Invocations programme *It Go Have To Adjust. On Language As Parasite* at SAVVY Contemporary, Berlin.

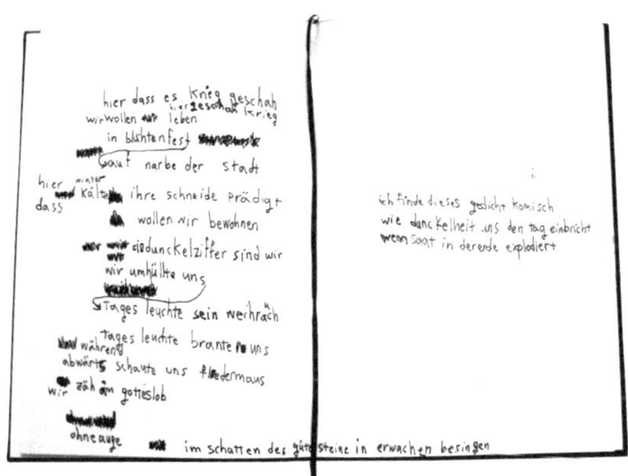

Pages from *glossolalie, automatic writing*, 2008-ongoing. Courtesy: the artist

WORKS

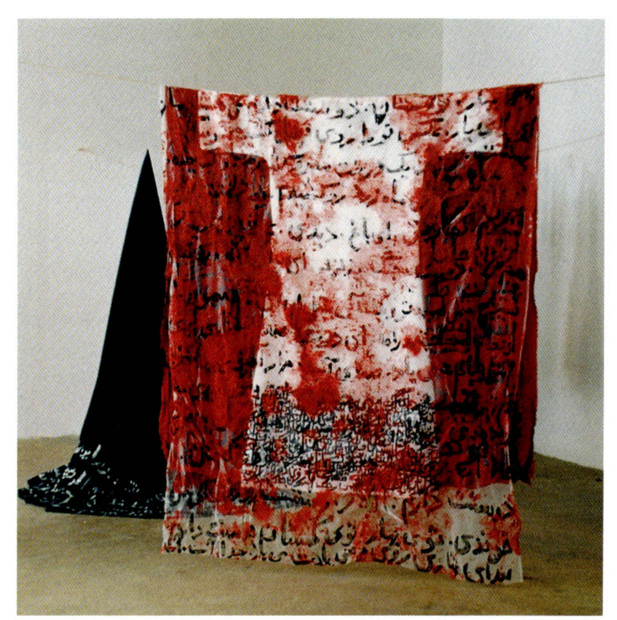

mobile garden/continental shift, 2000

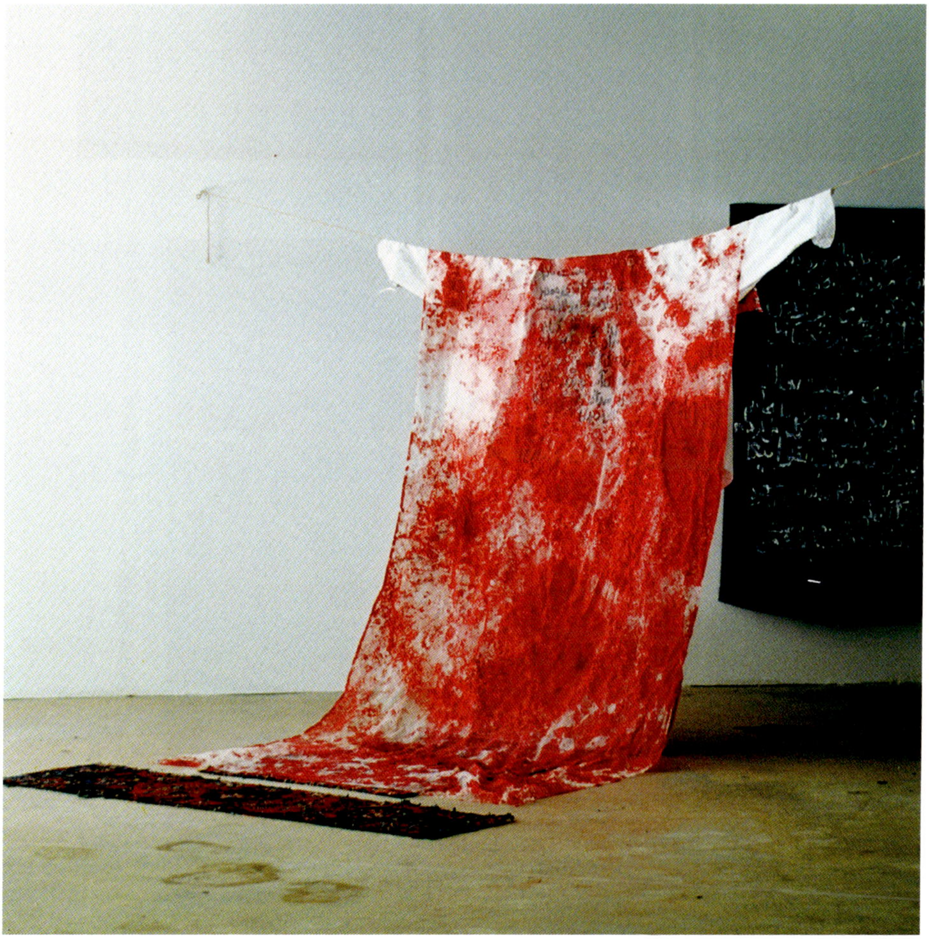

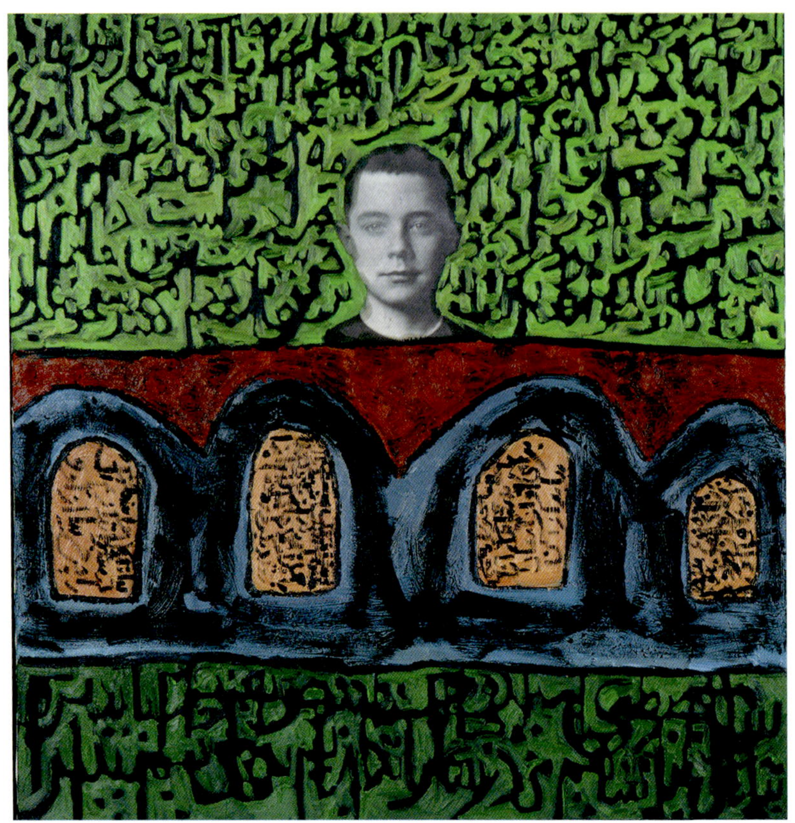

ein sohn, 1996

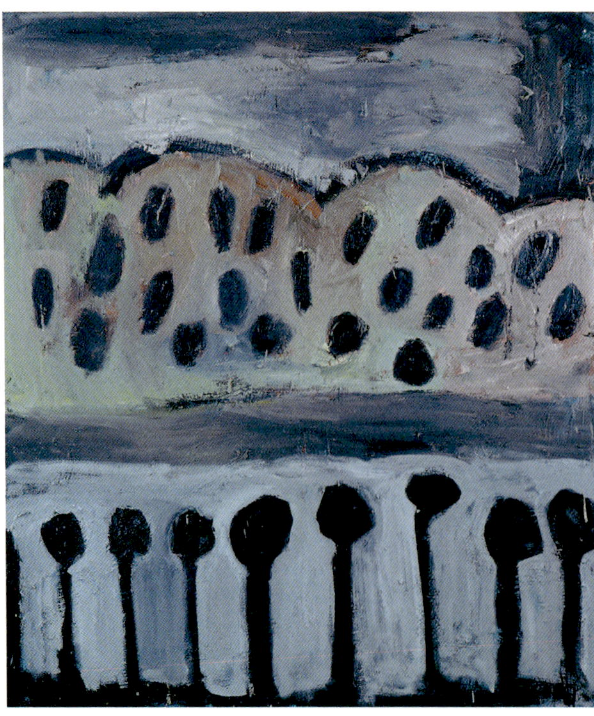

untitled, 1994

untitled, 1994

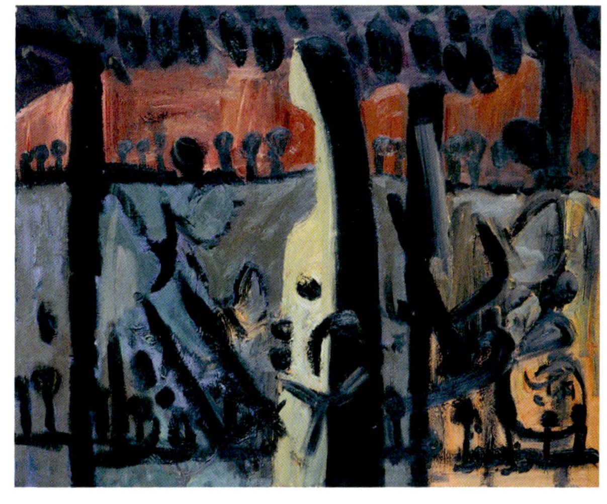

untitled, 1994

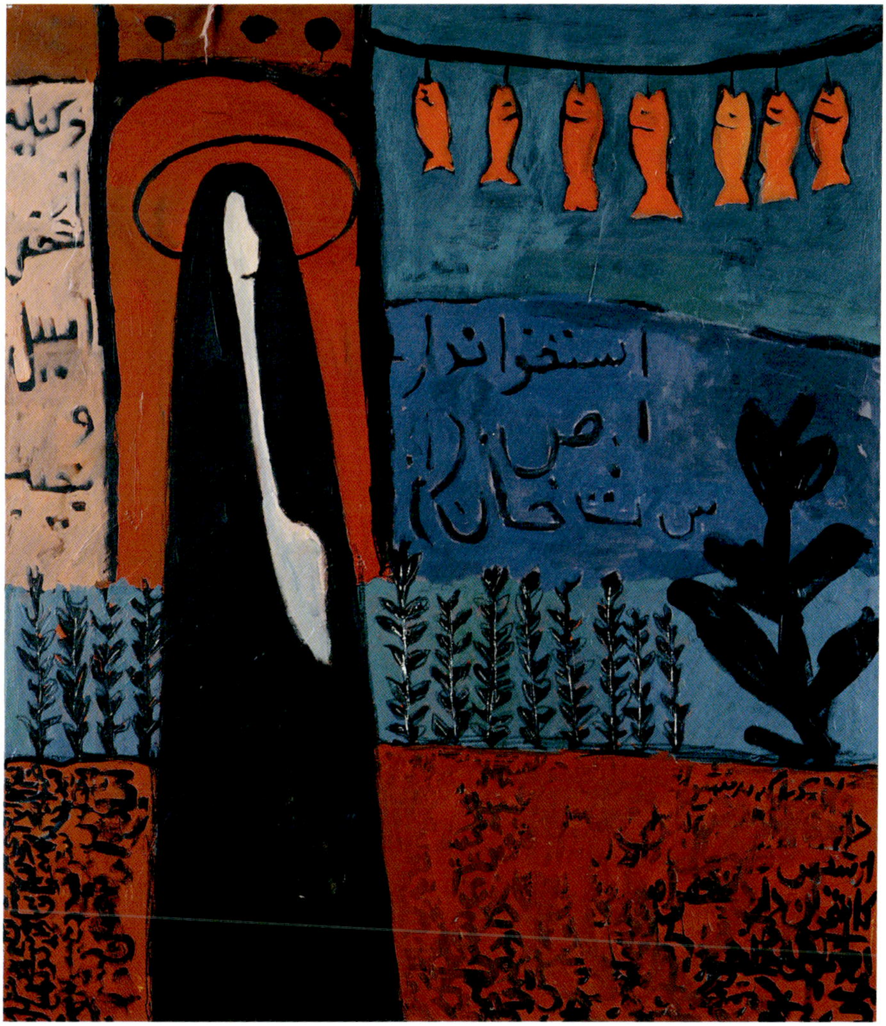

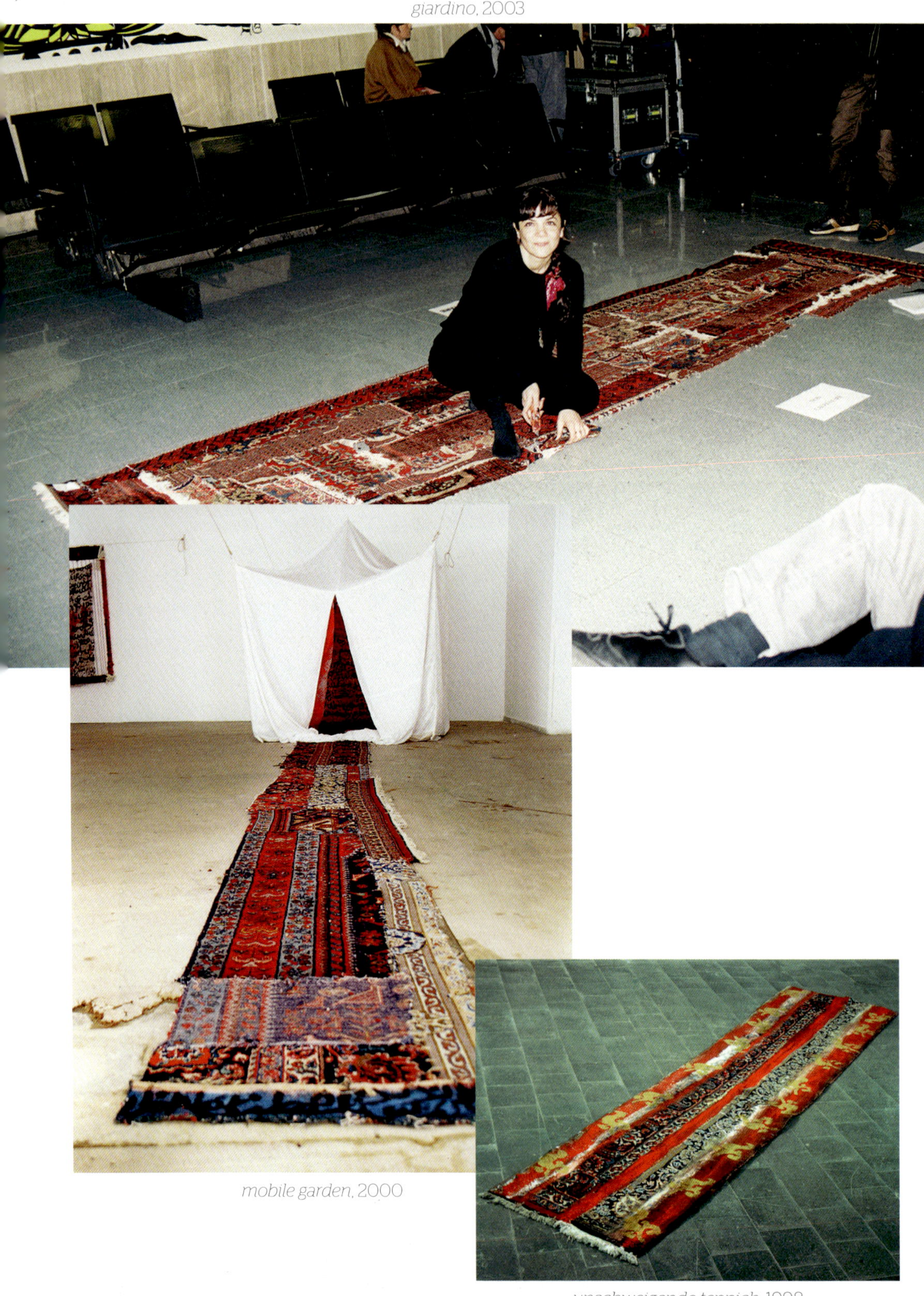

giardino, 2003

mobile garden, 2000

unschweigende teppich, 1998

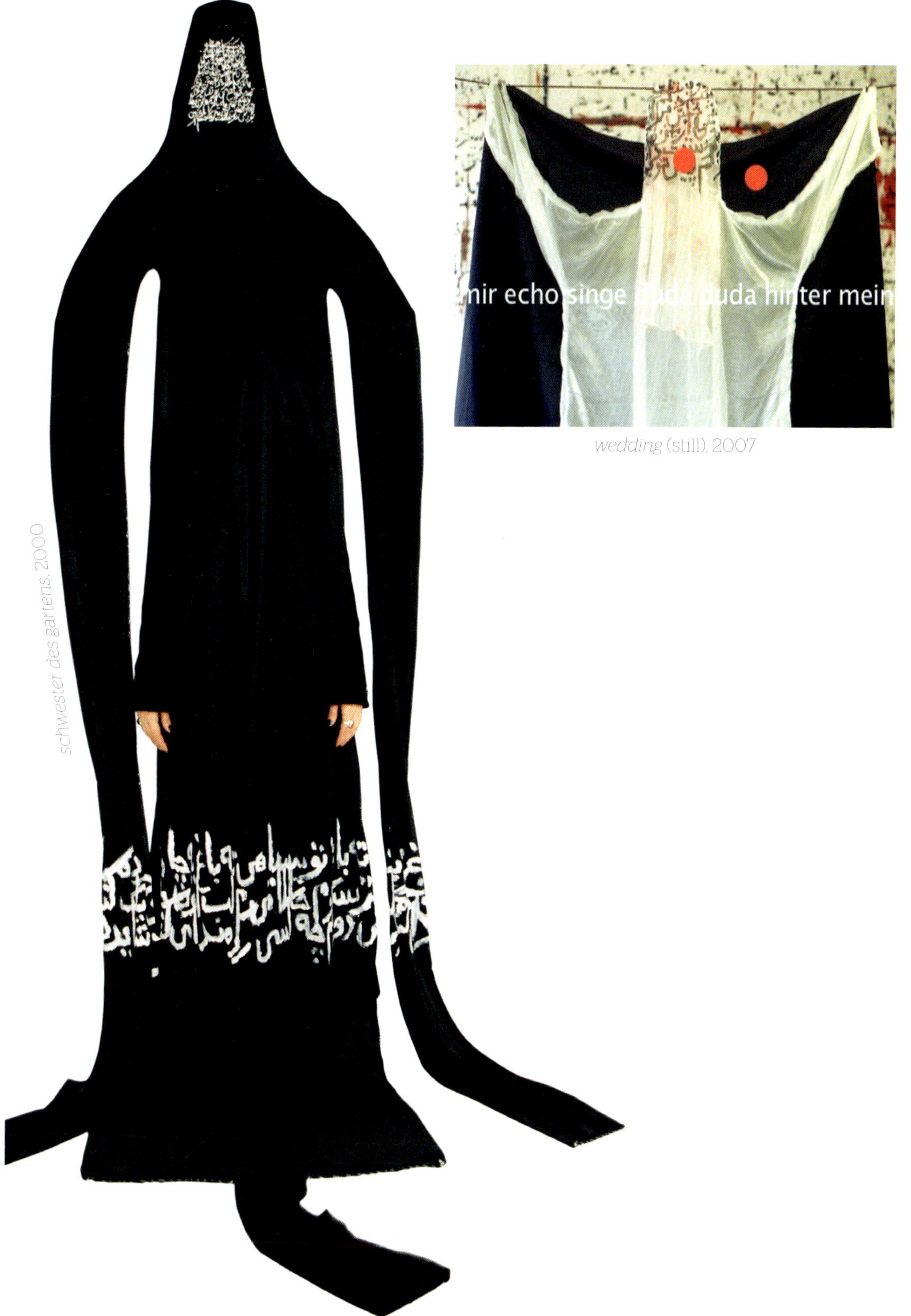

schwester des gartens, 2000

wedding (still), 2007

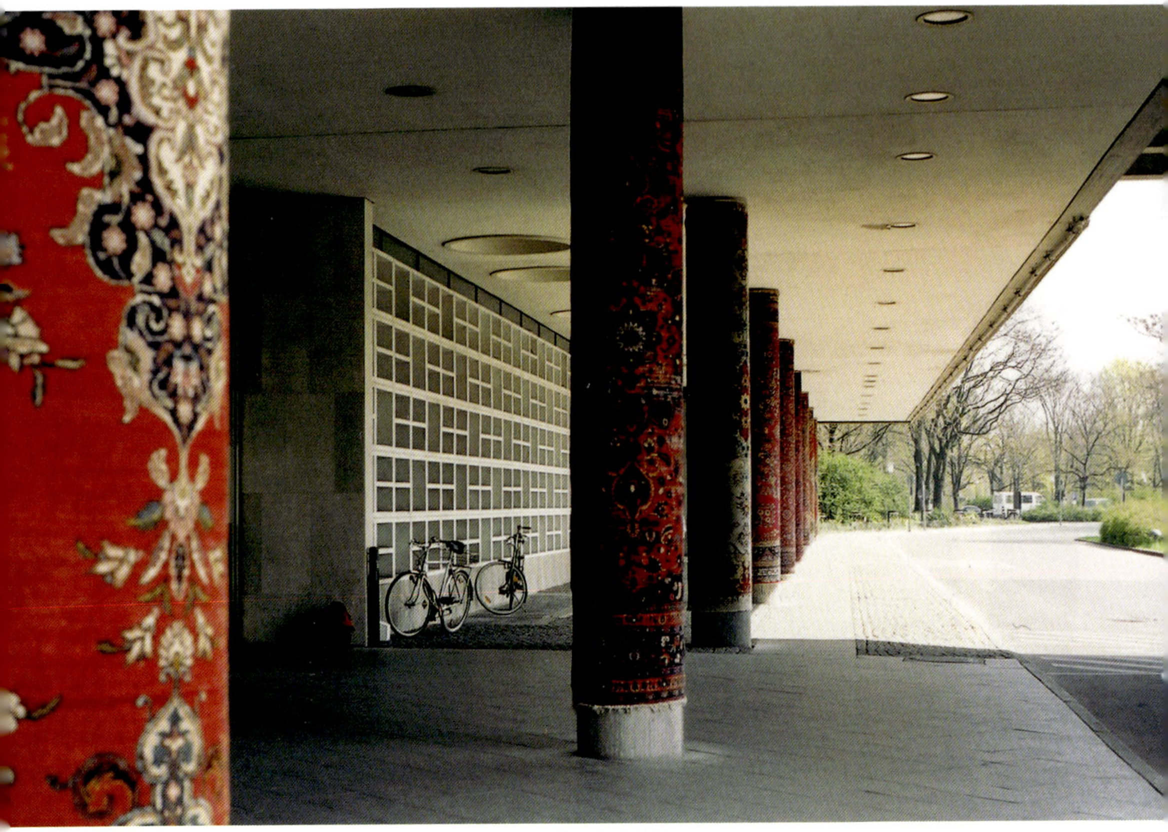

garten/bagh, 2004

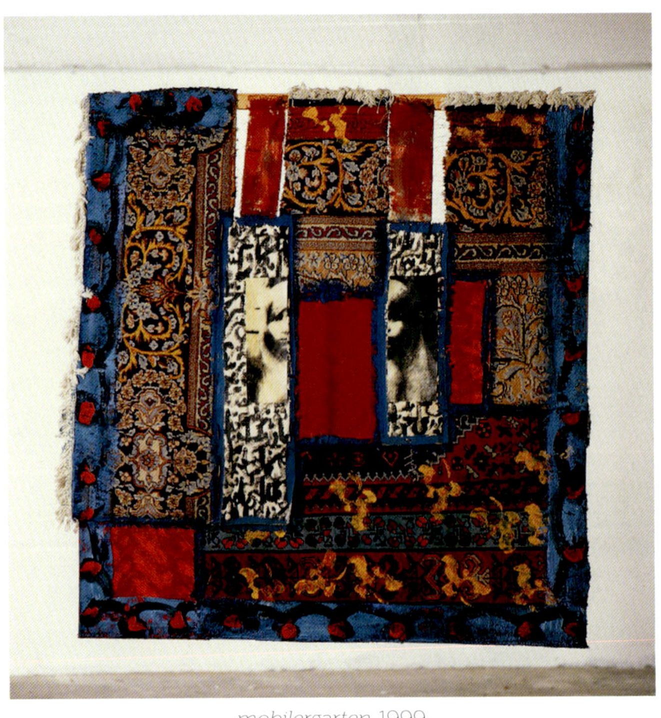

mobilergarten, 1999

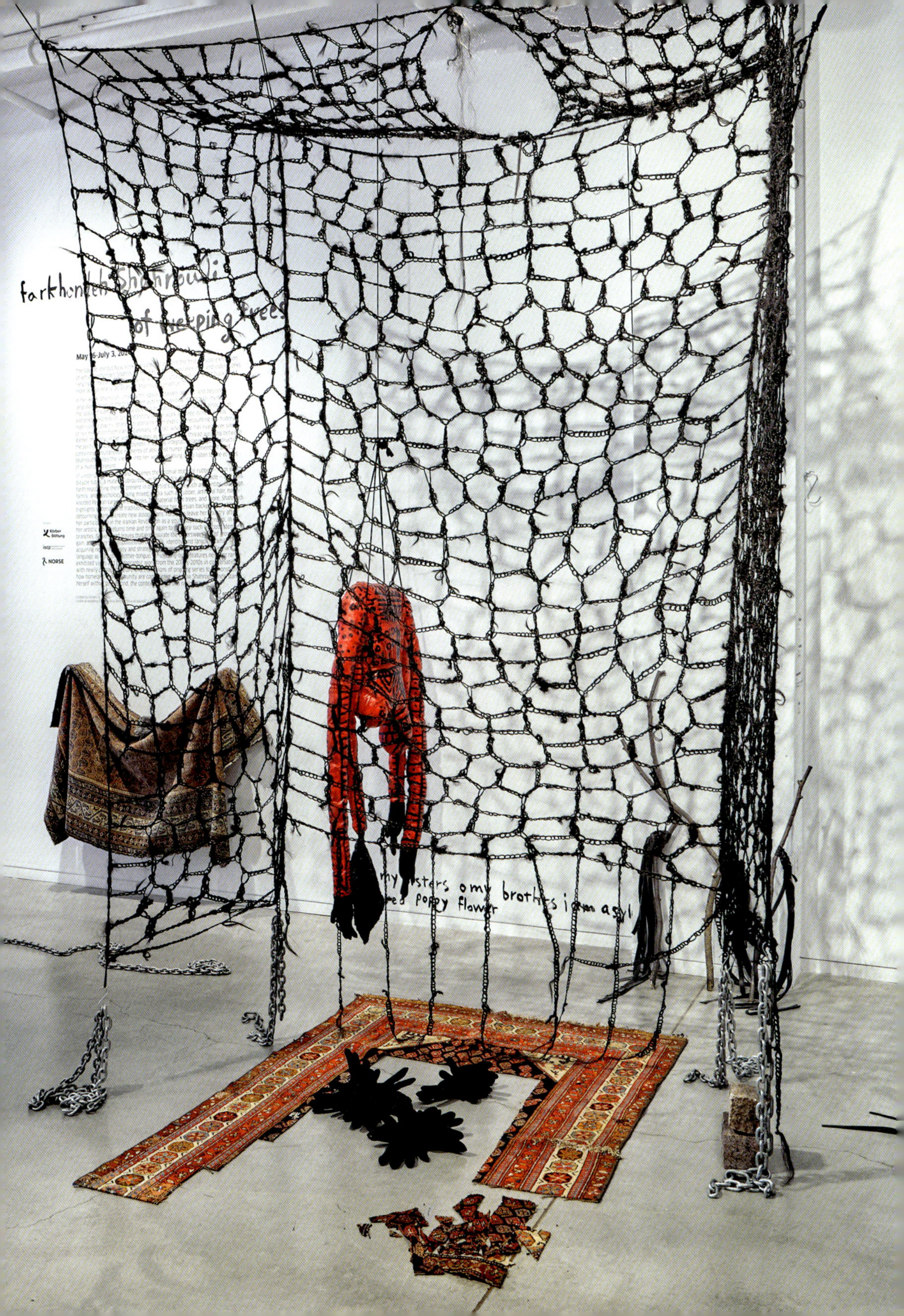

farkhondeh shahroudi
of weeping trees
May 16-July 3, 202
my sisters o my brothers i am asyl
red poppy flower

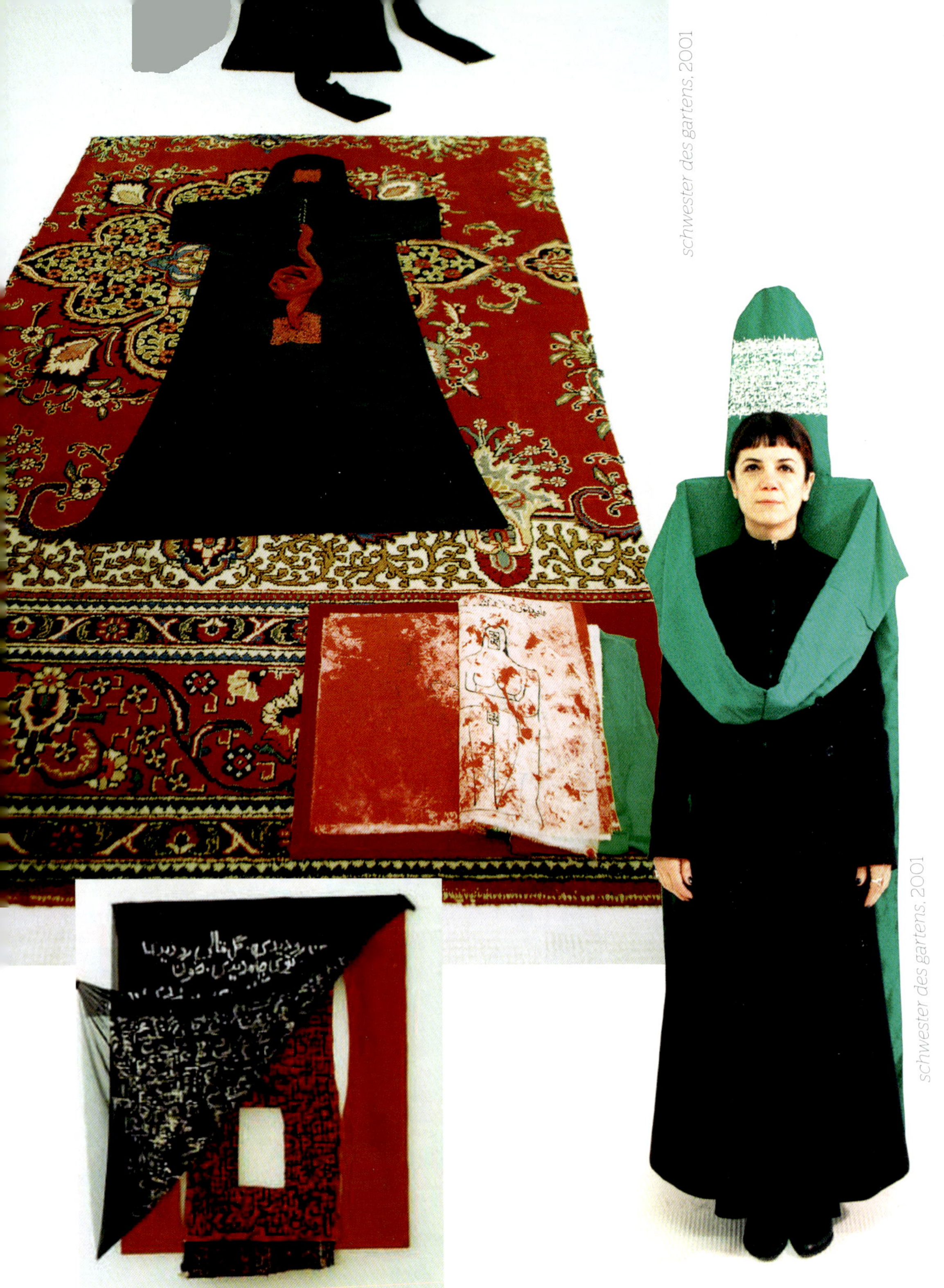

mobile garden, 2000

garden in the garden/madjnoun, 2003

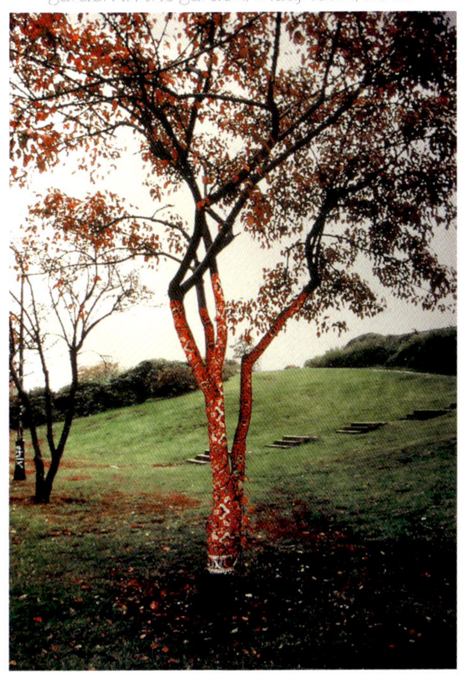

mobile garden/guluzar, 2005

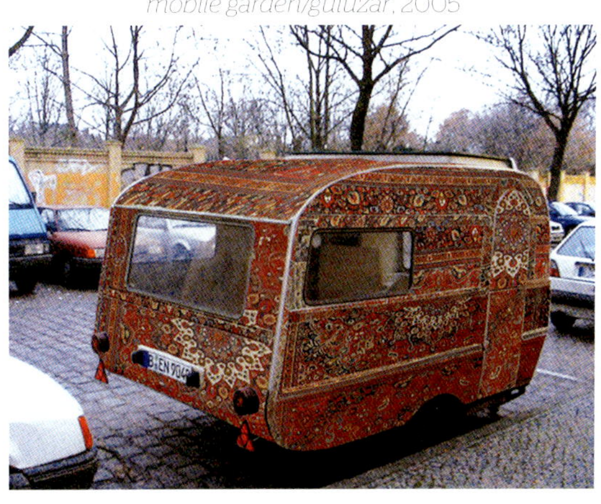

garten/bagh, 2004

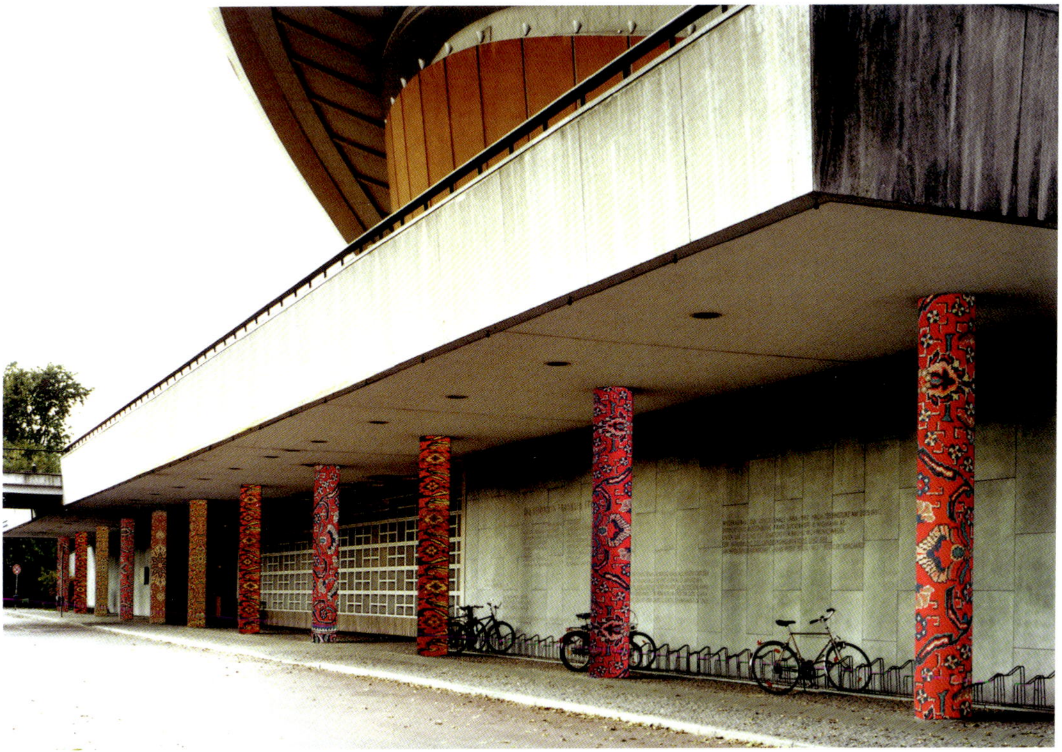

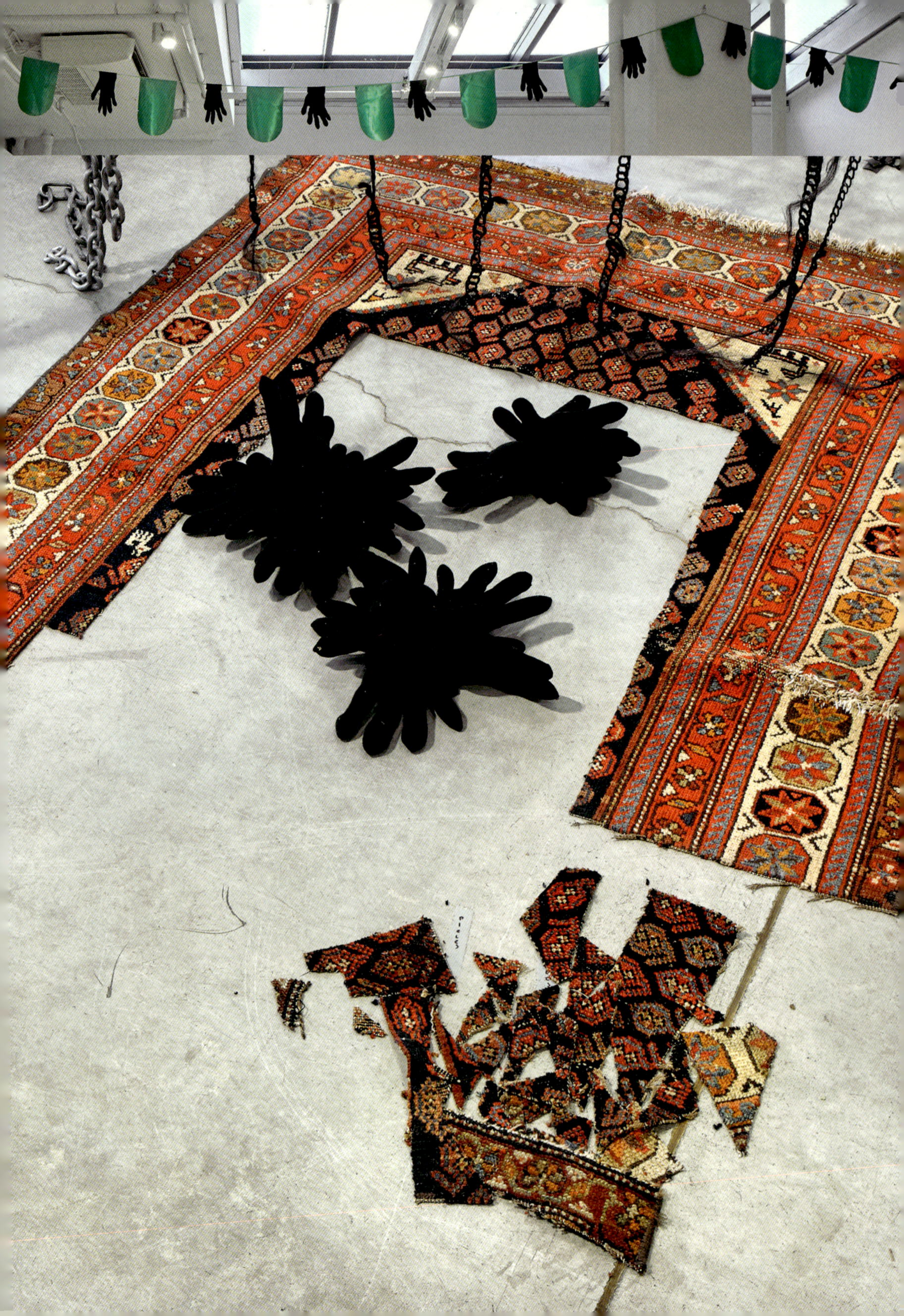

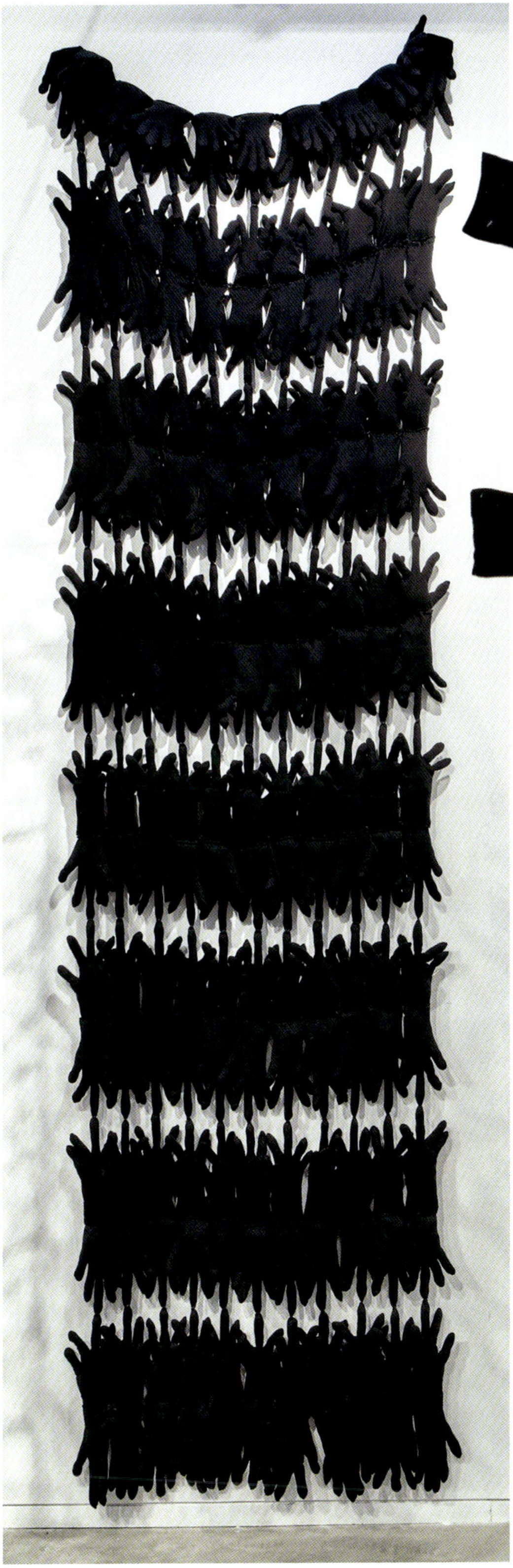

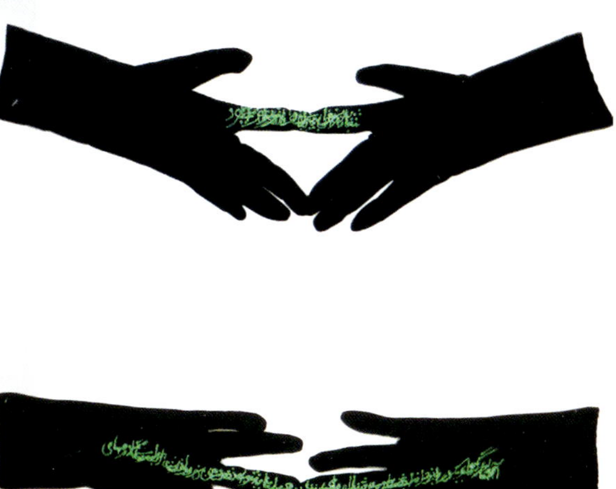

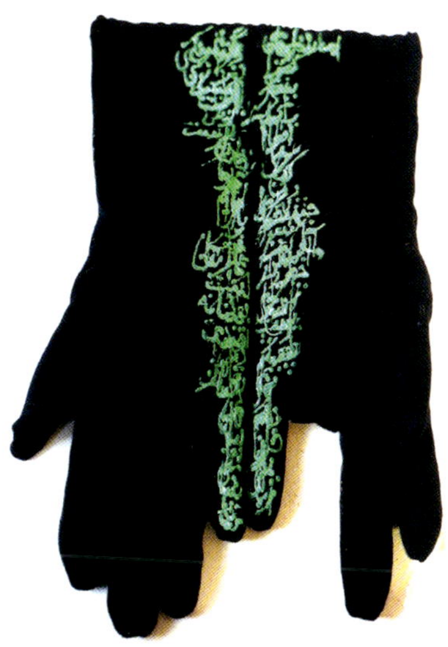

880 fingers, 2024

taubstumm, 2003-04

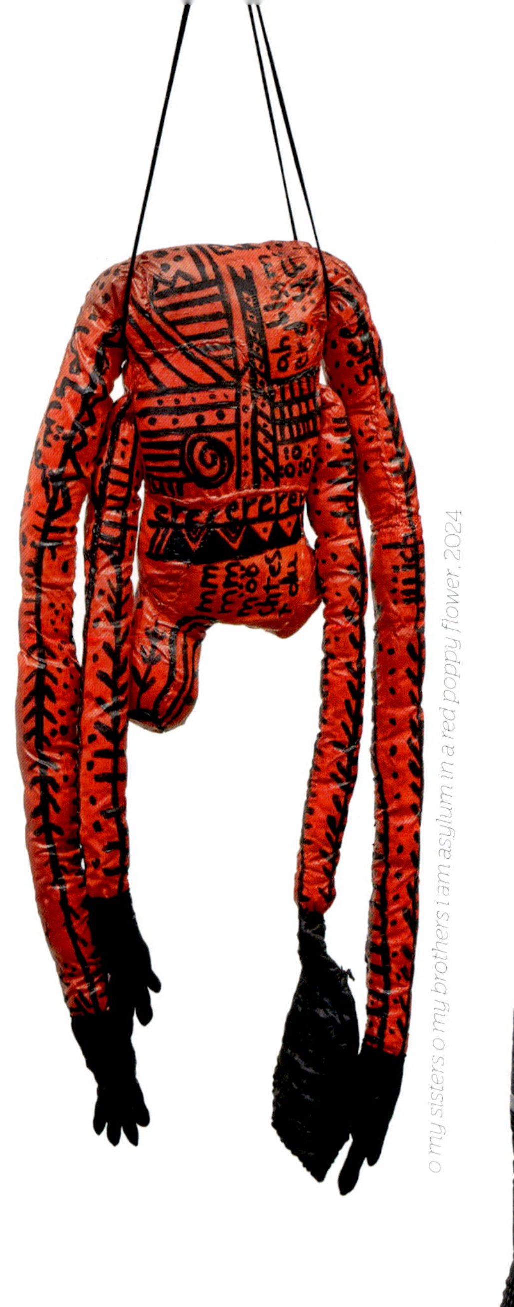

o my sisters o my brothers i am asylum in a red poppy flower. 2024

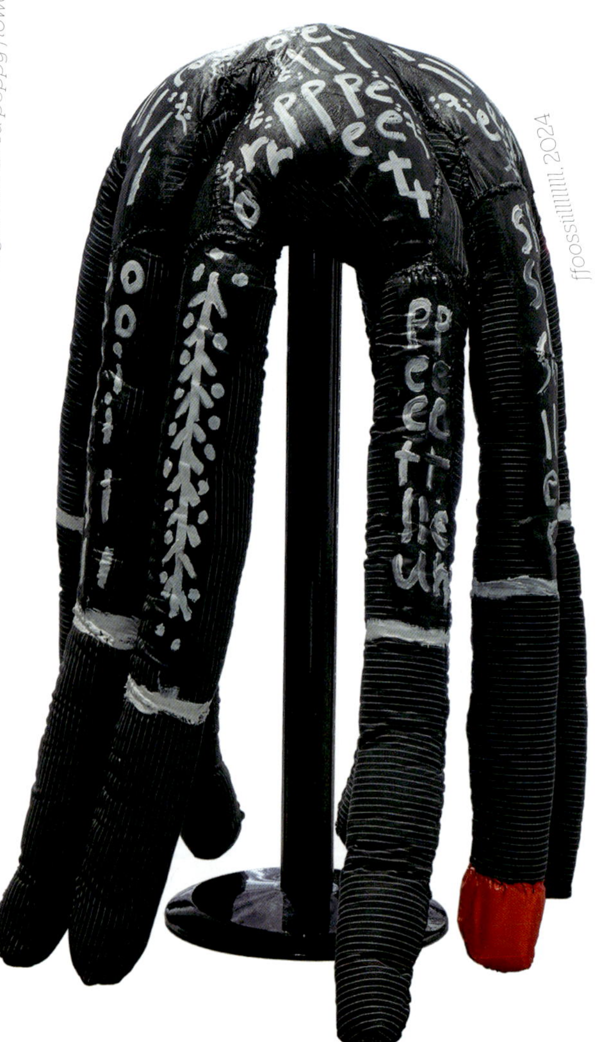

ffoossiillllll. 2024

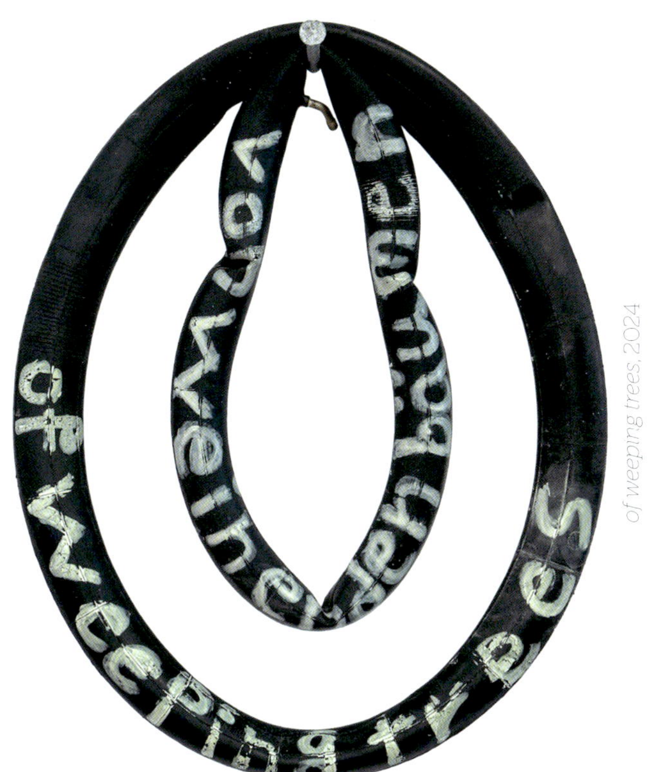

of weeping trees, 2024

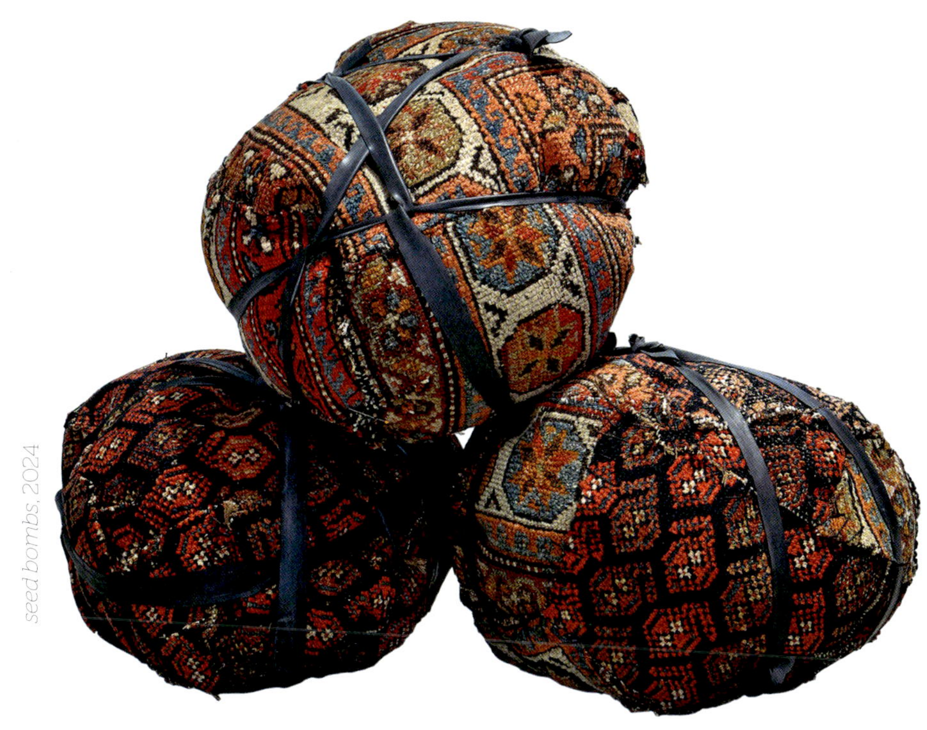

seed bombs, 2024

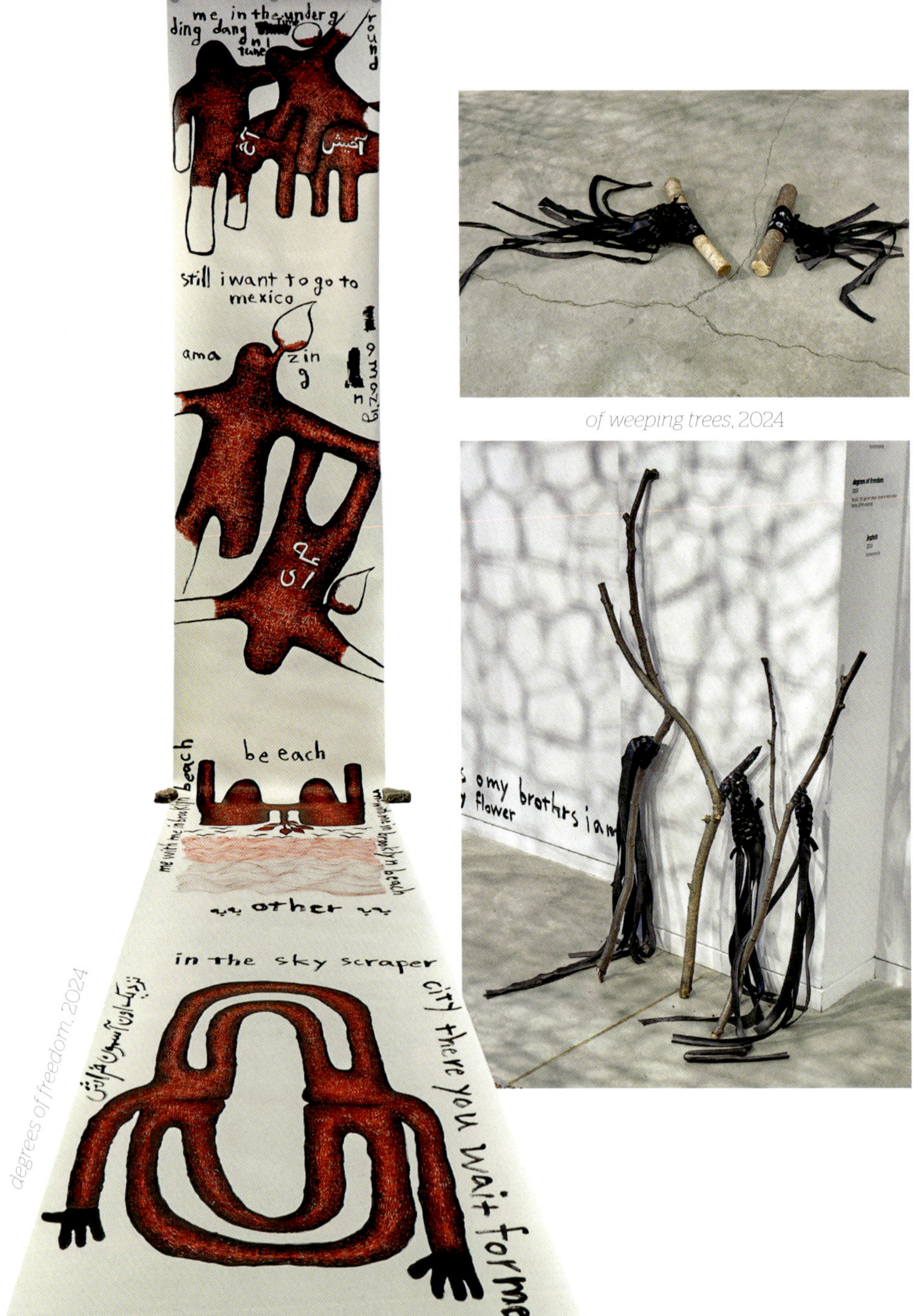
me in the under g
ding dang
round
still i want to go to mexico
ama
zin
g
be each
other
in the sky scraper
city there you wait for me
o my brothrs i am
flower
degrees of freedom, 2024
of weeping trees, 2024

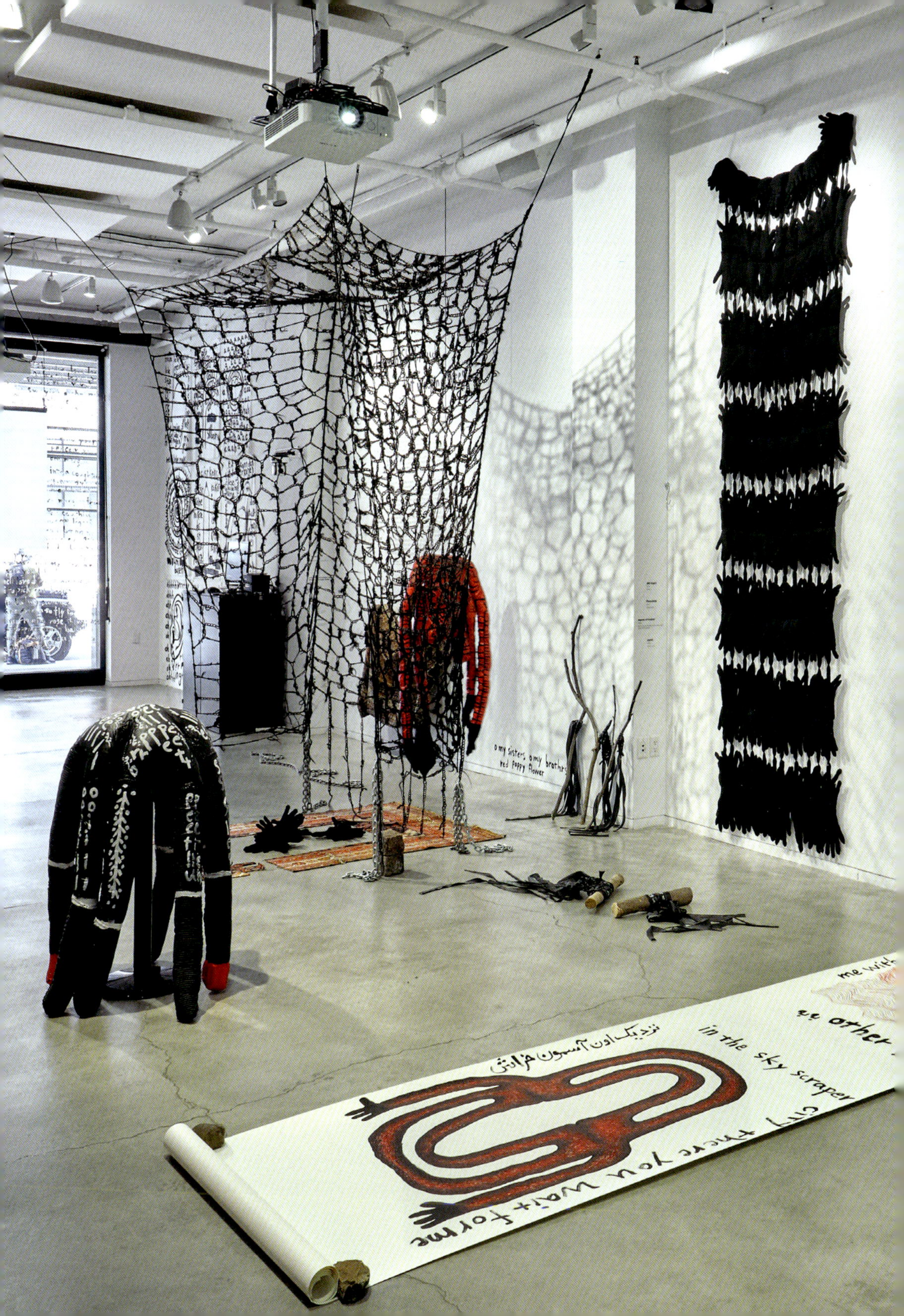

o my sisters, o my brothers
red poppy flower
in the sky scraper
نزدیک اون آسمون خراش
there you wait for me
me with
ee other

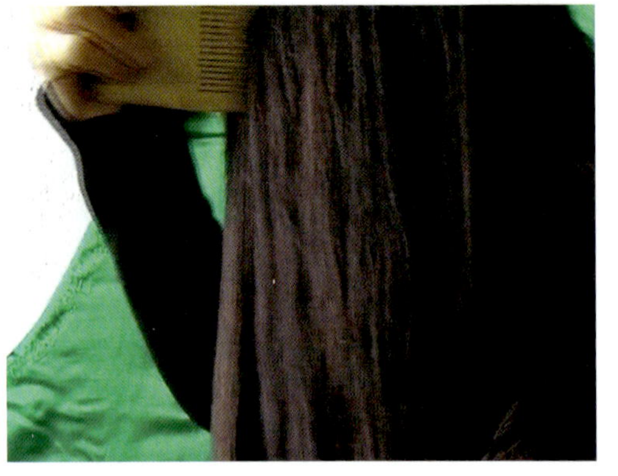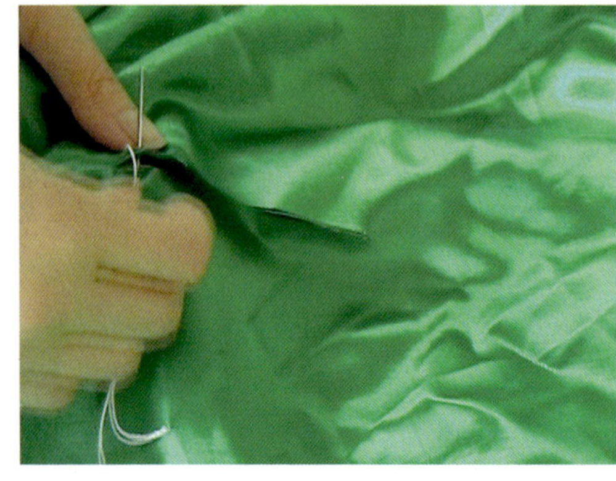
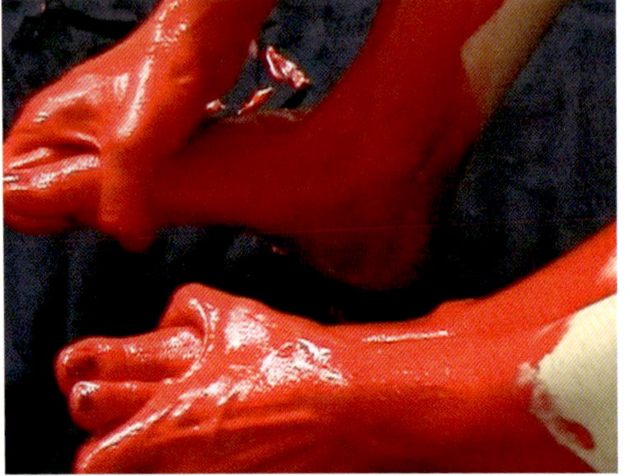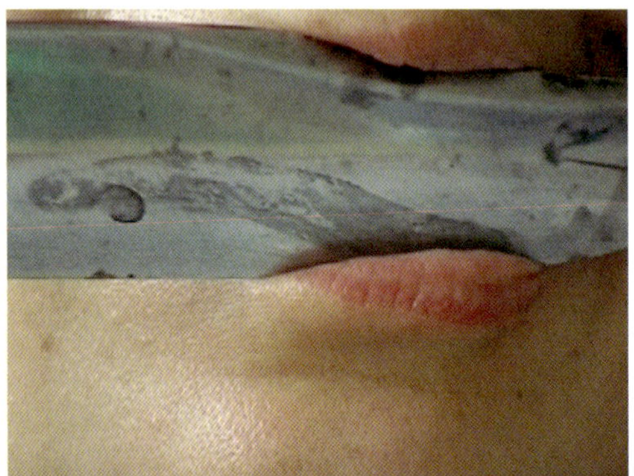
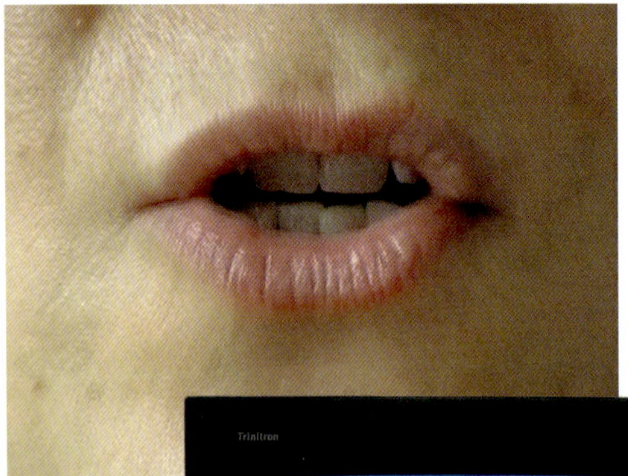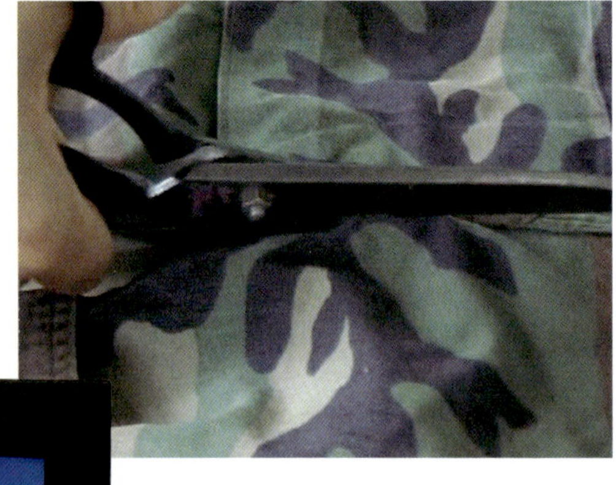

tab (stills), 2003-05

hallucination, 2001

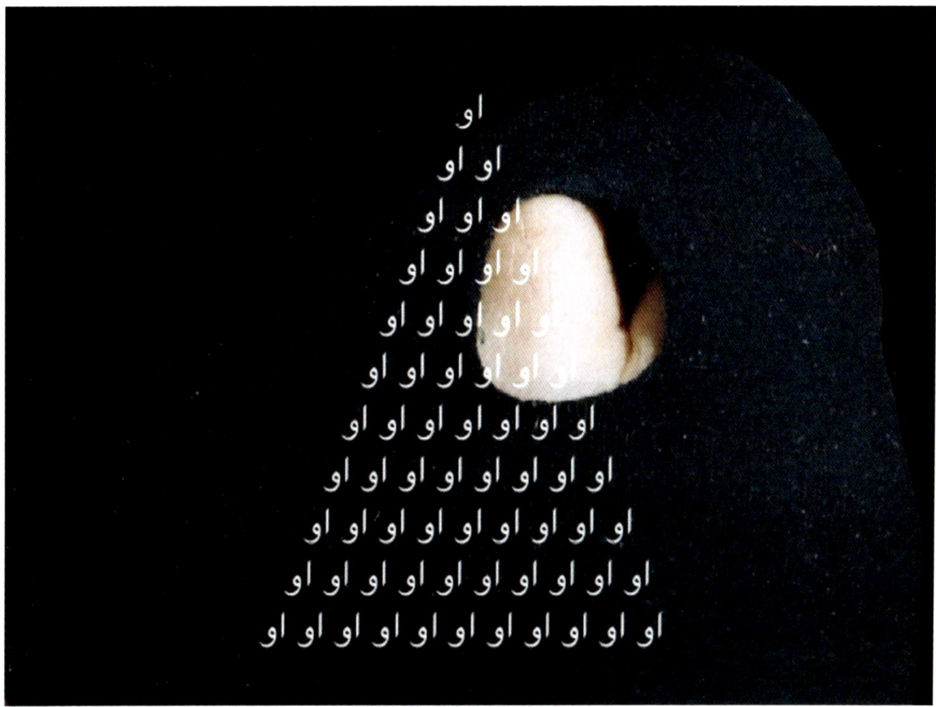

ou (still), 2012

glossolalia, automatic writing, 2008-10

checkmate, 2010

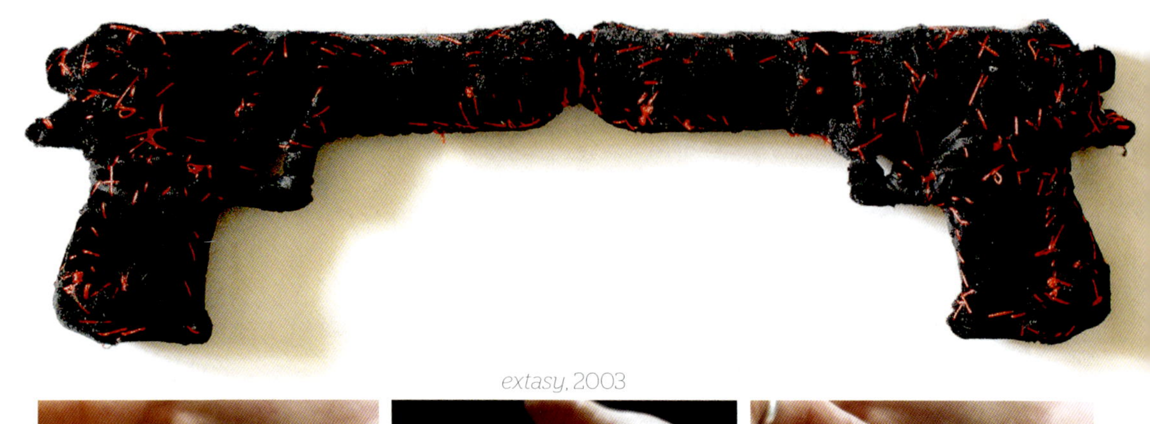

extasy, 2003

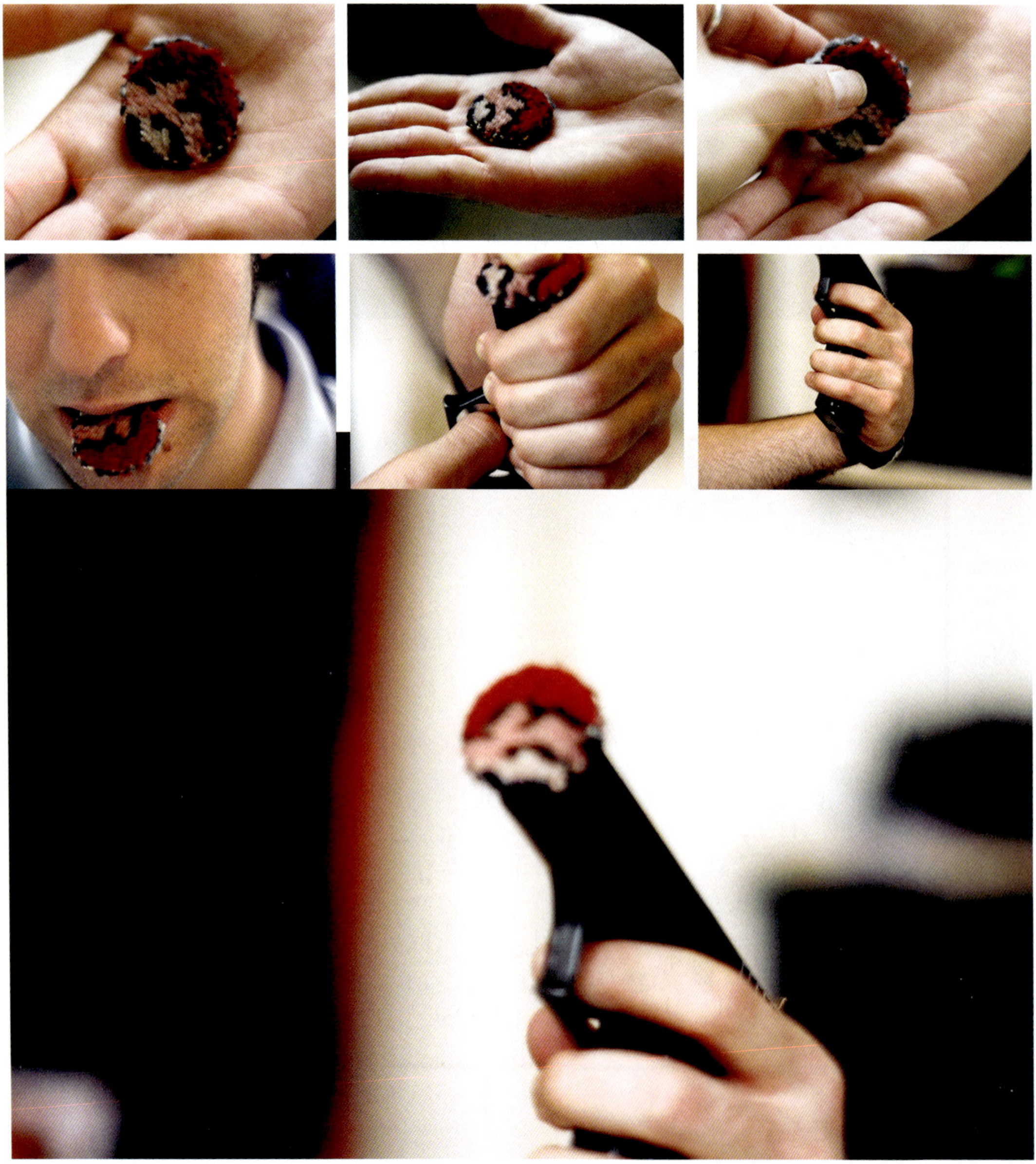

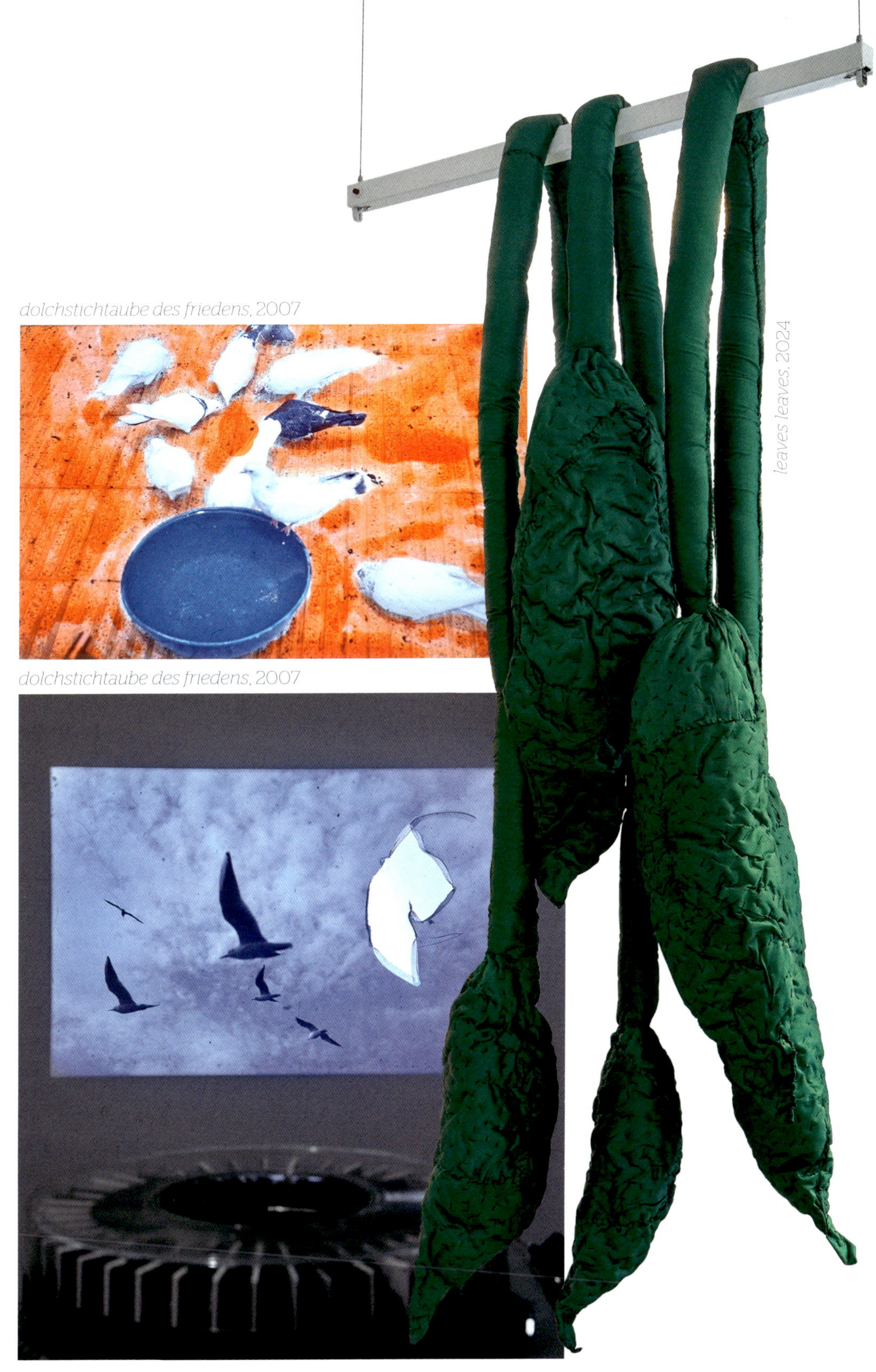

dolchstichtaube des friedens, 2007
dolchstichtaube des friedens, 2007
leaves leaves, 2024

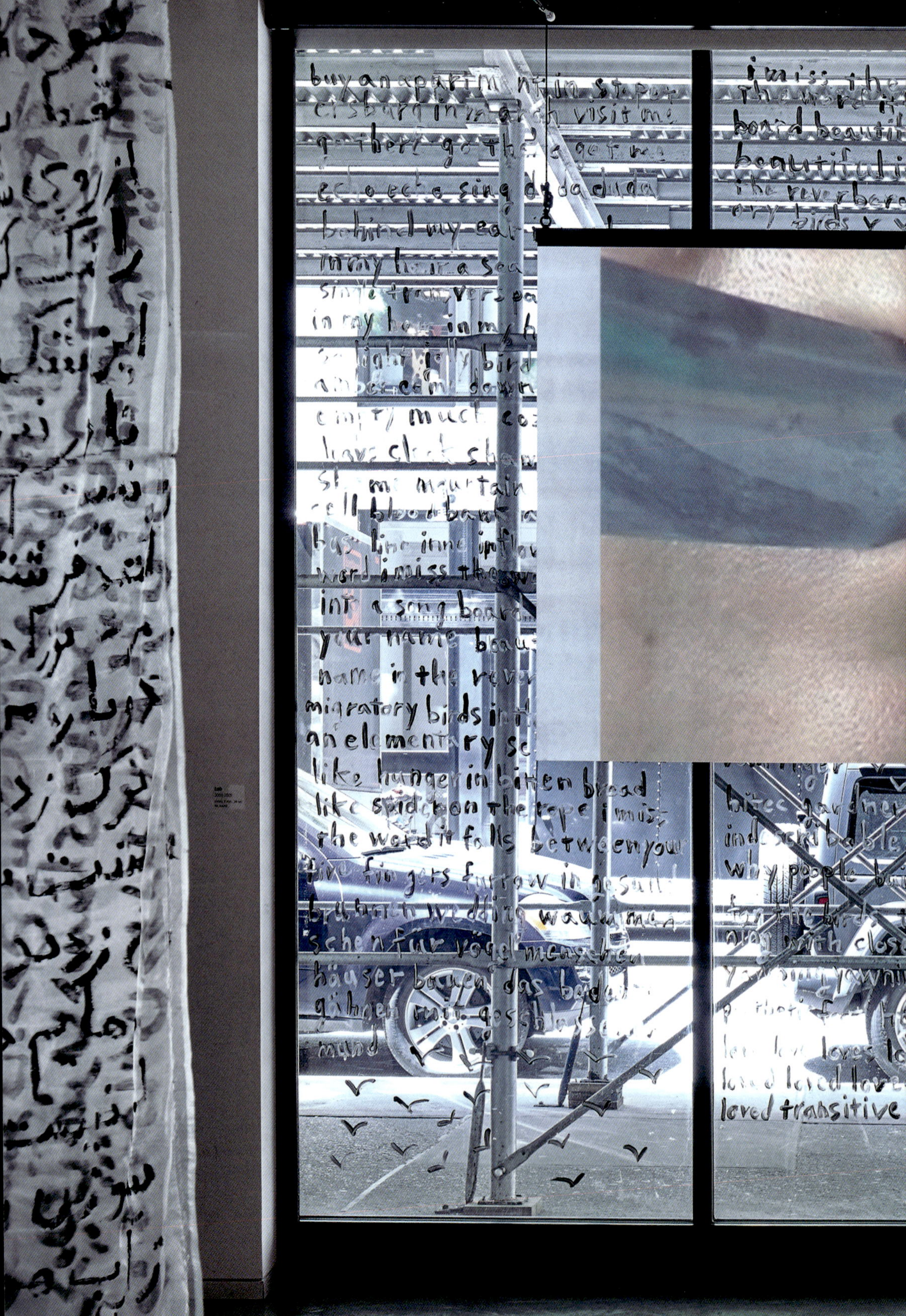

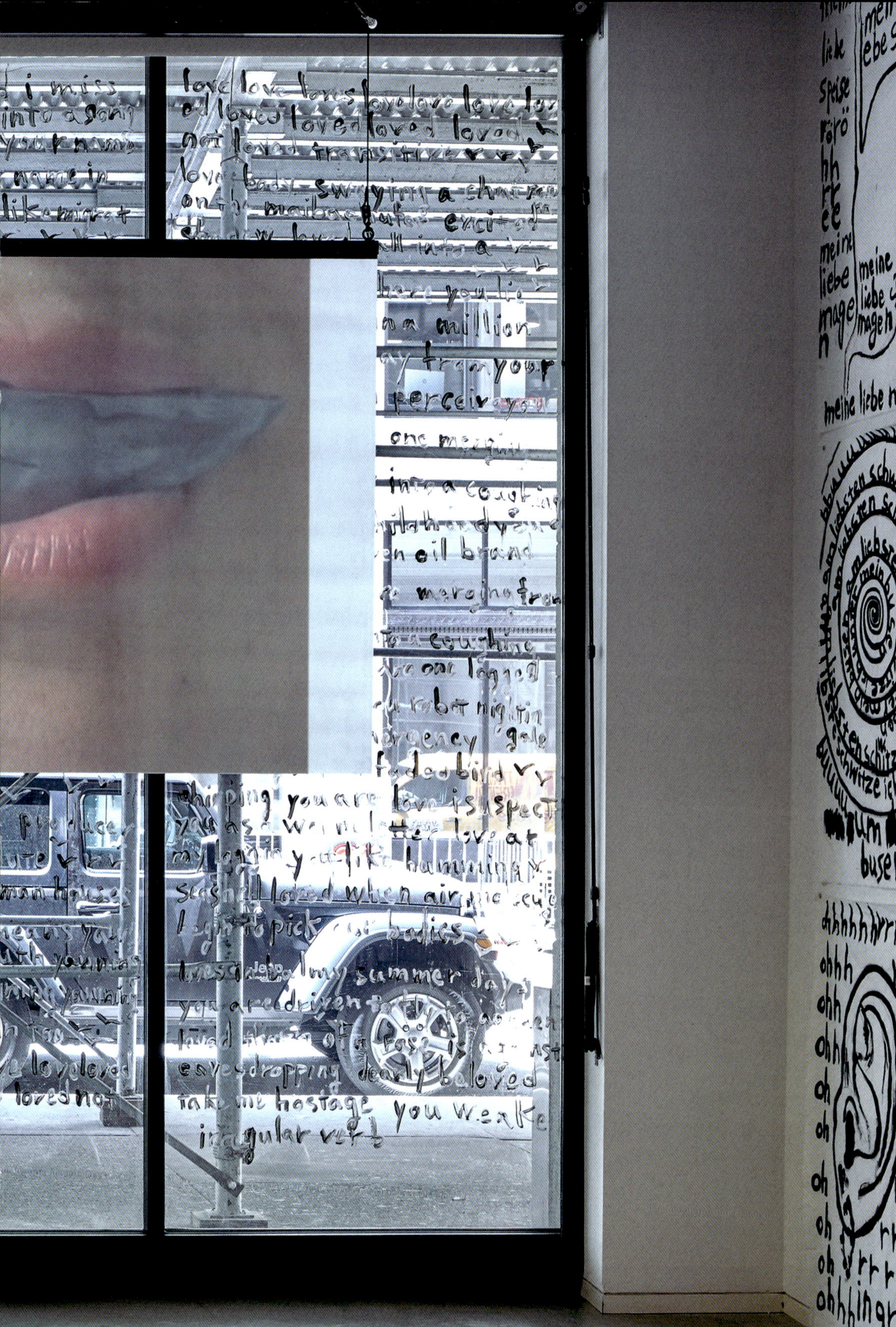

Farkhondeh Shahroudi's studio, Berlin, 2022

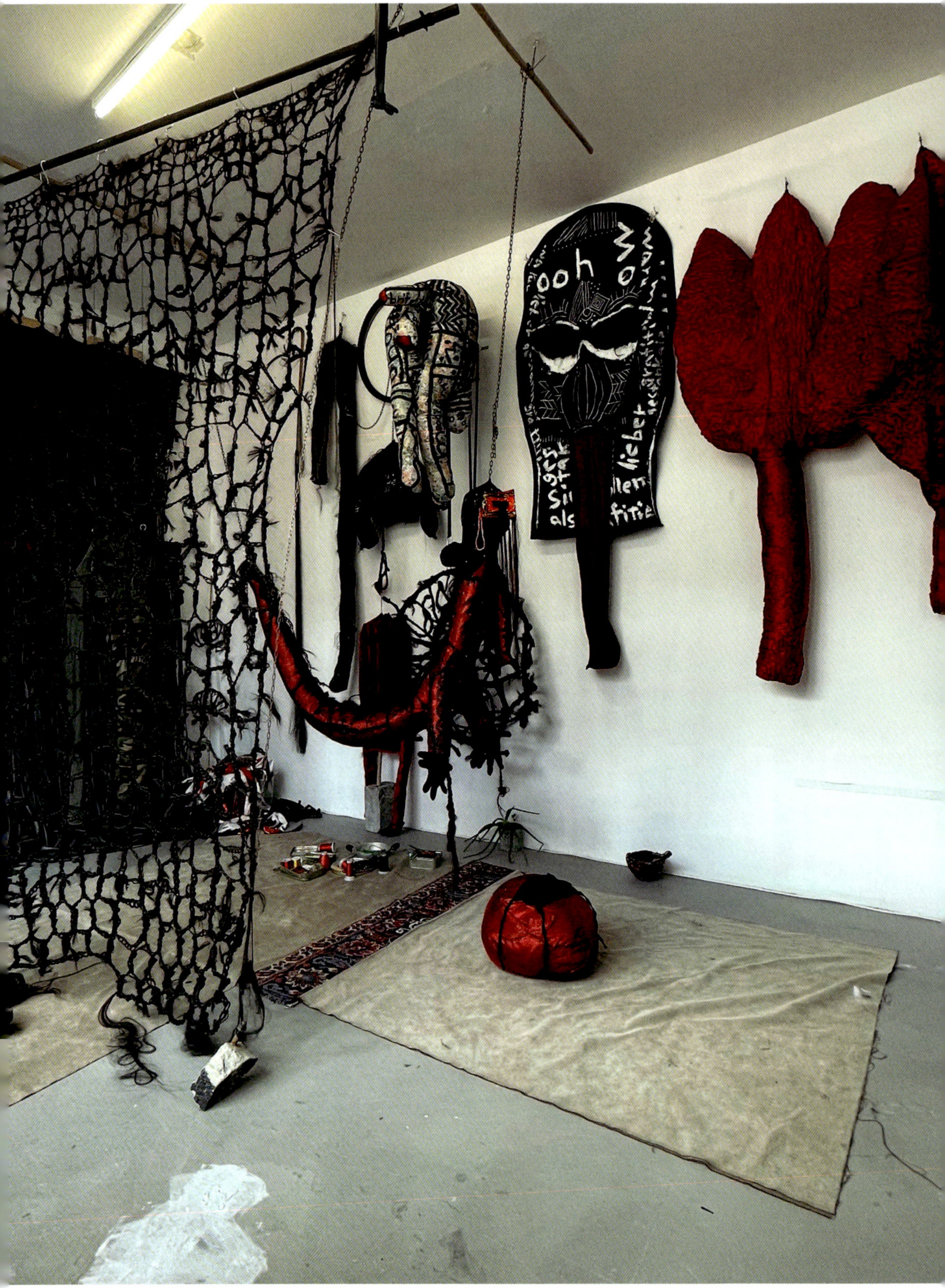

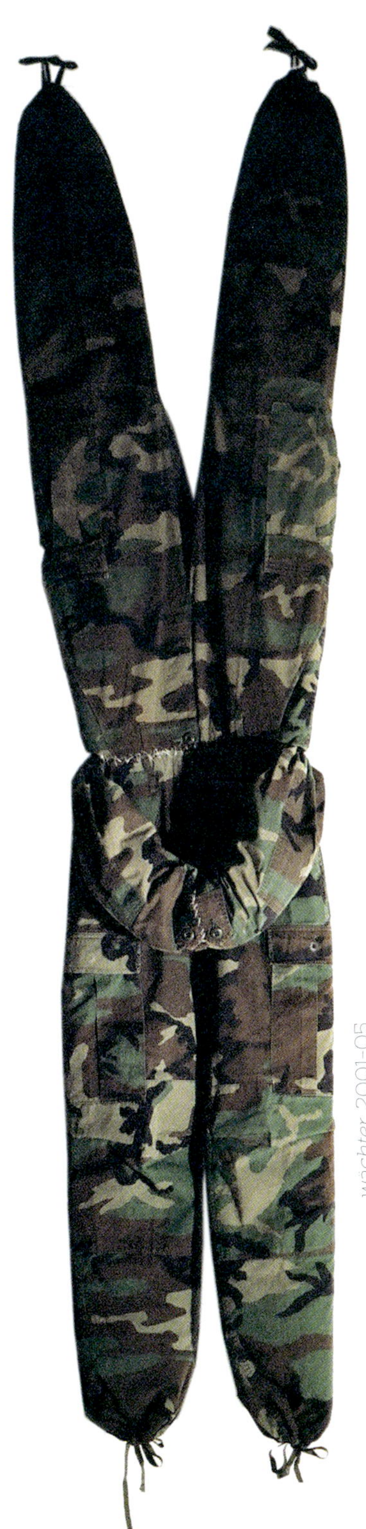

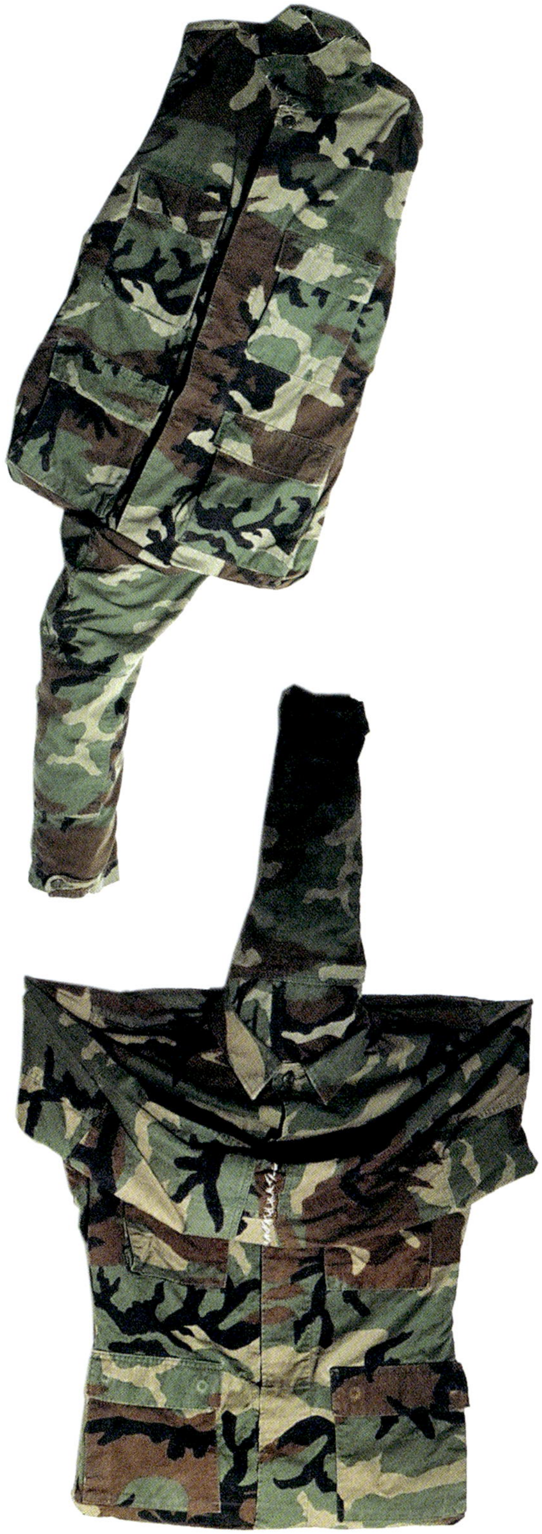

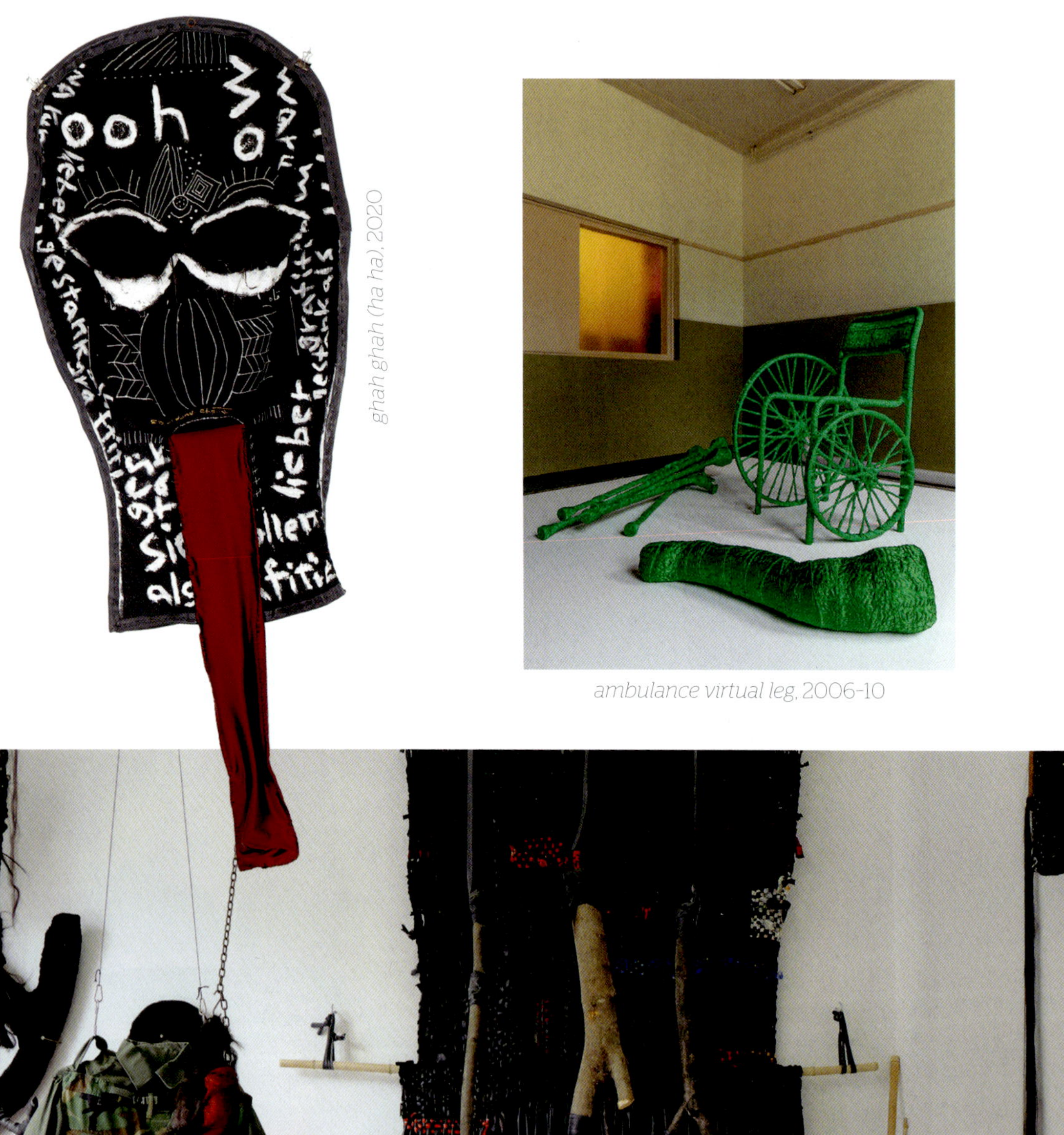

ghah ghah (ha ha), 2020

ambulance virtual leg, 2006-10

Farkhondeh Shahroudi's studio, Berlin, 2022

oh, 2021; seed bomb, 2021; antiflag (anna mermaid), 2021/performative poetics of matter, 2021

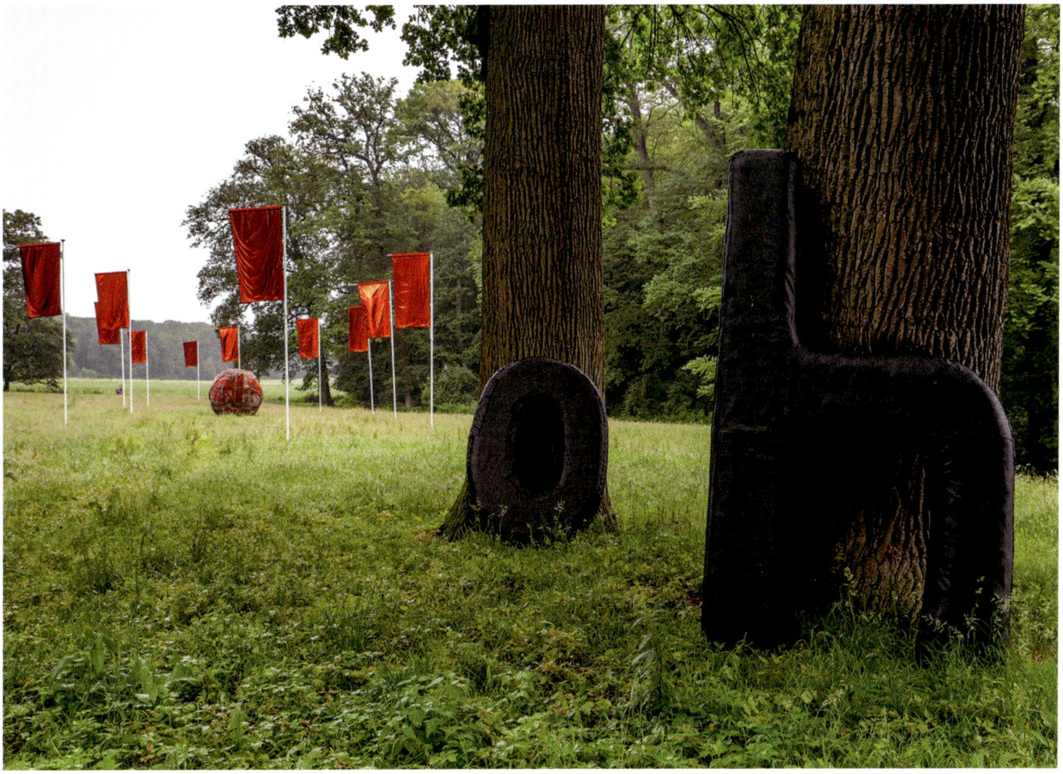

seed bomb, 2021; antiflag (anna mermaid), 2021/performative poetics of matter, 2021

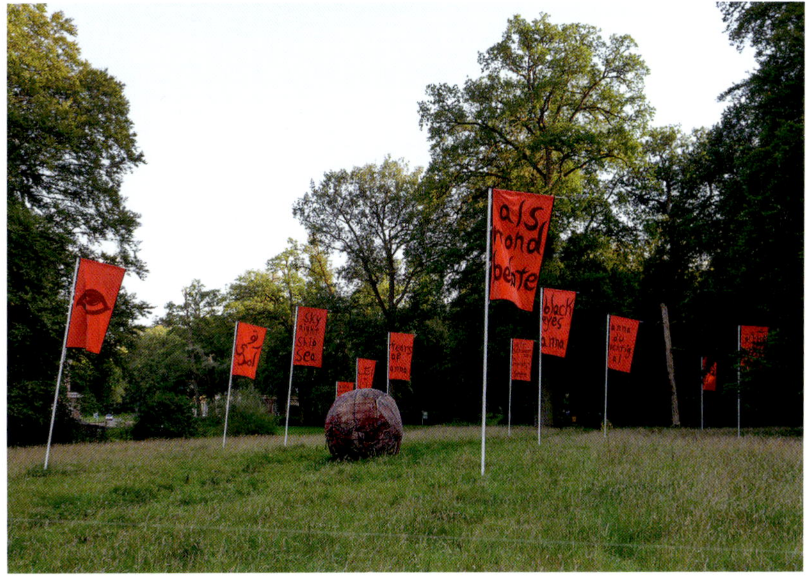

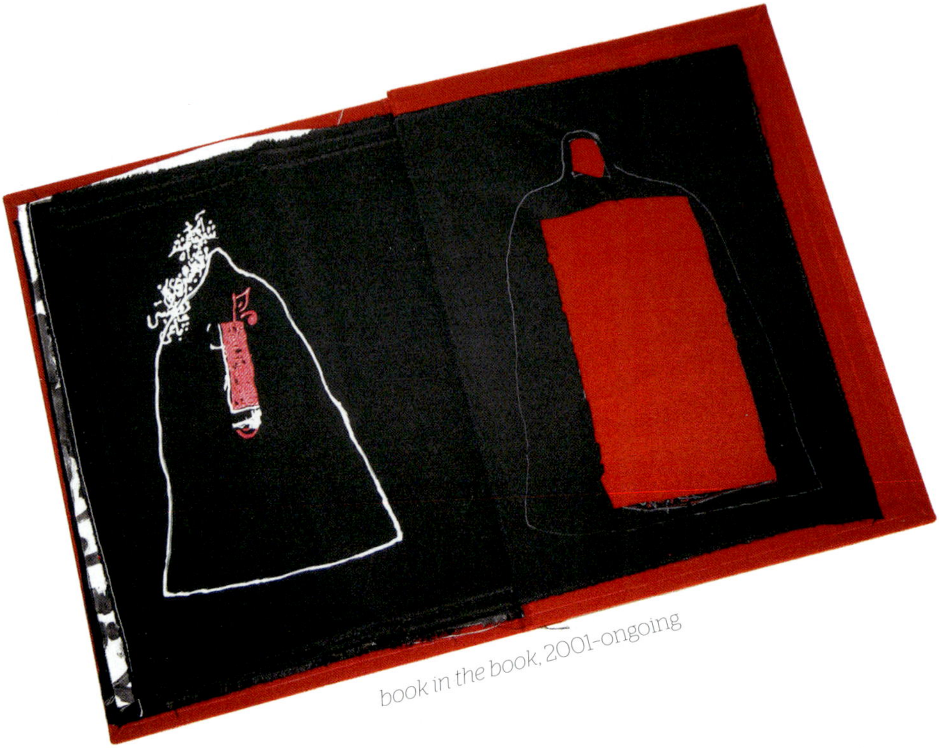

book in the book, 2001-ongoing

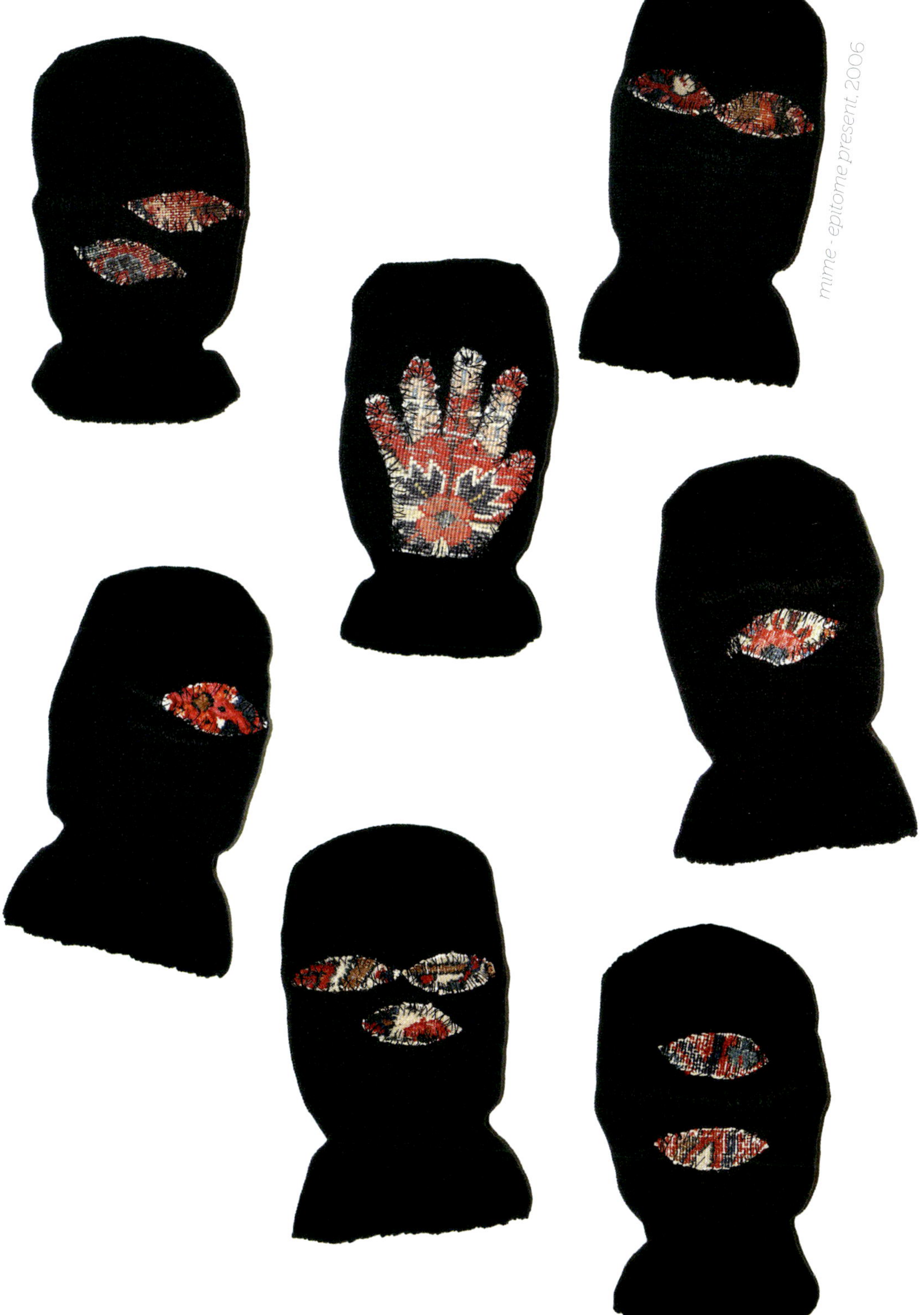

mime - epitome present. 2006

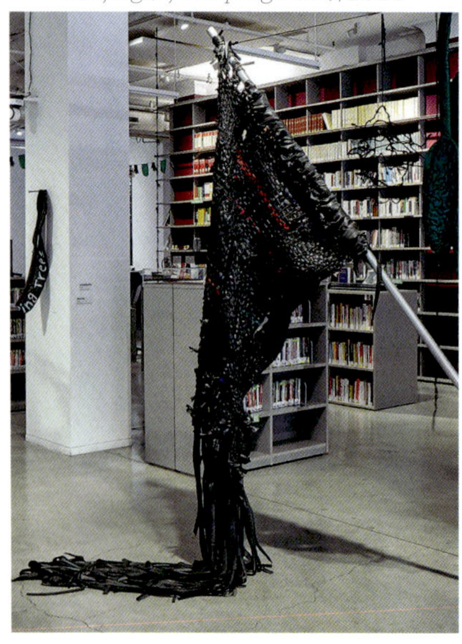

antiflag (of weeping trees), 2024

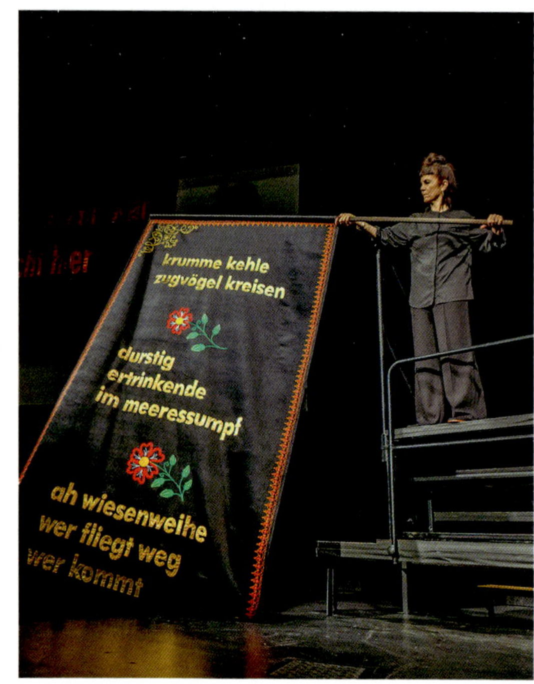

antiflag (sky is no ones ground), 2019

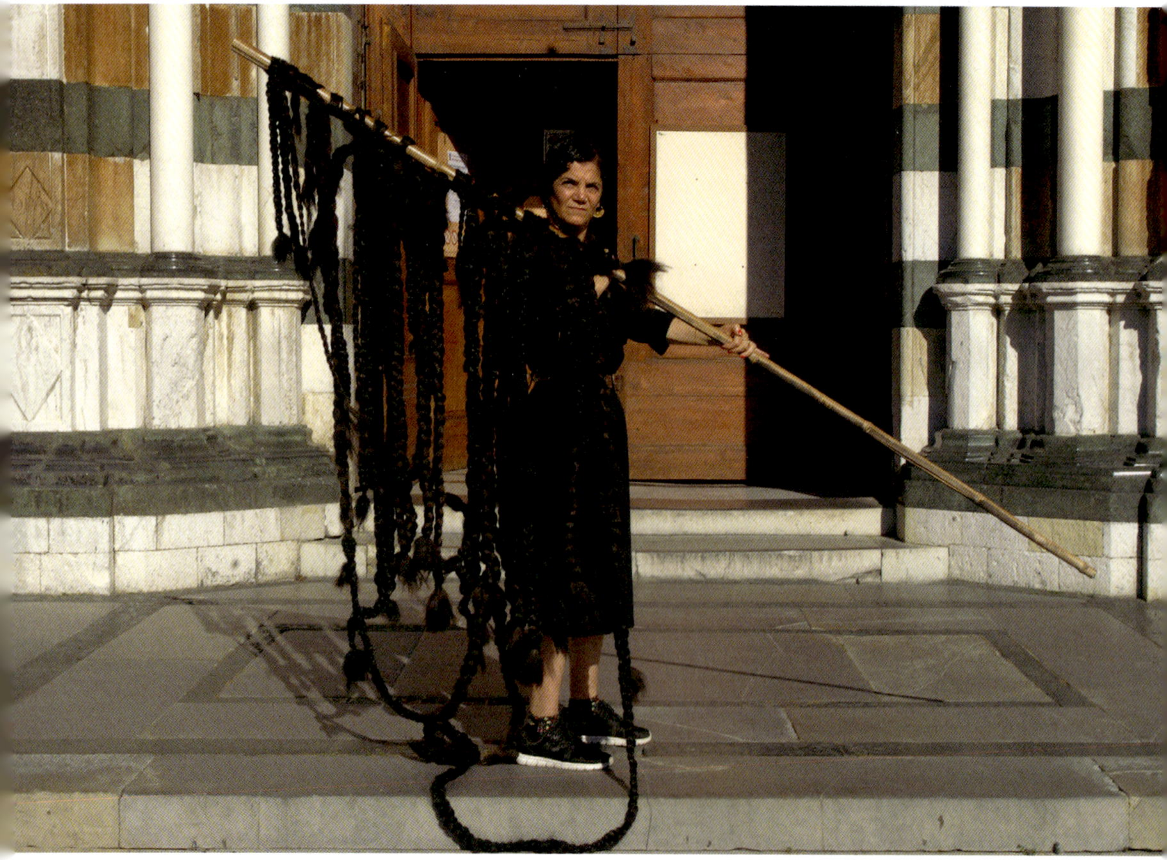

antiflag (hair demonstration), 2017

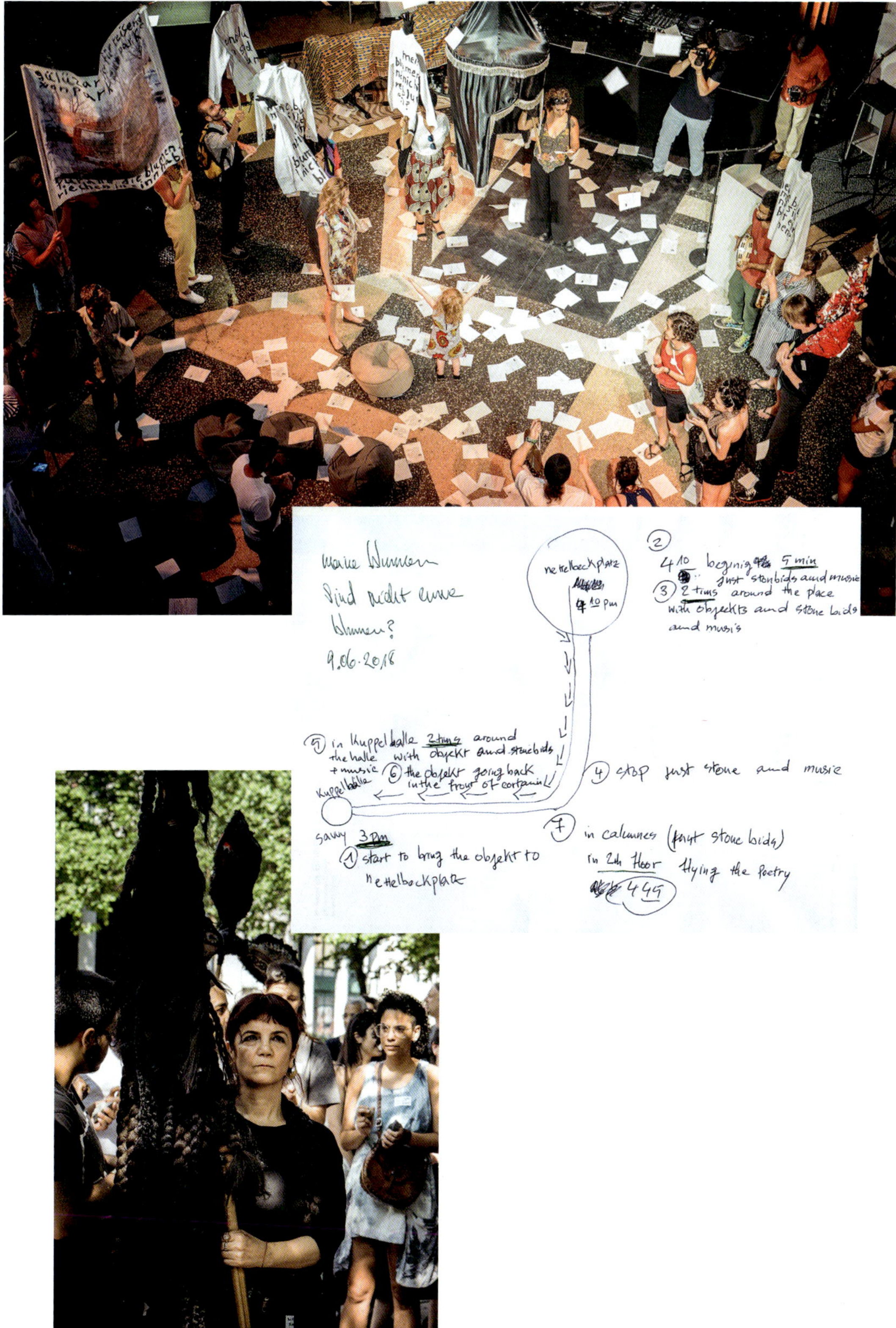

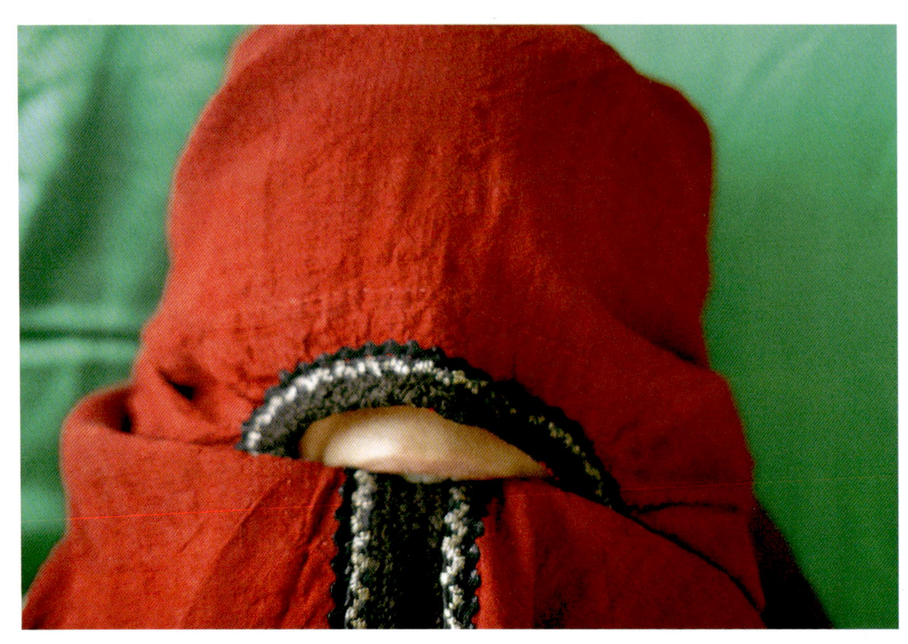

ausfinger, 2003

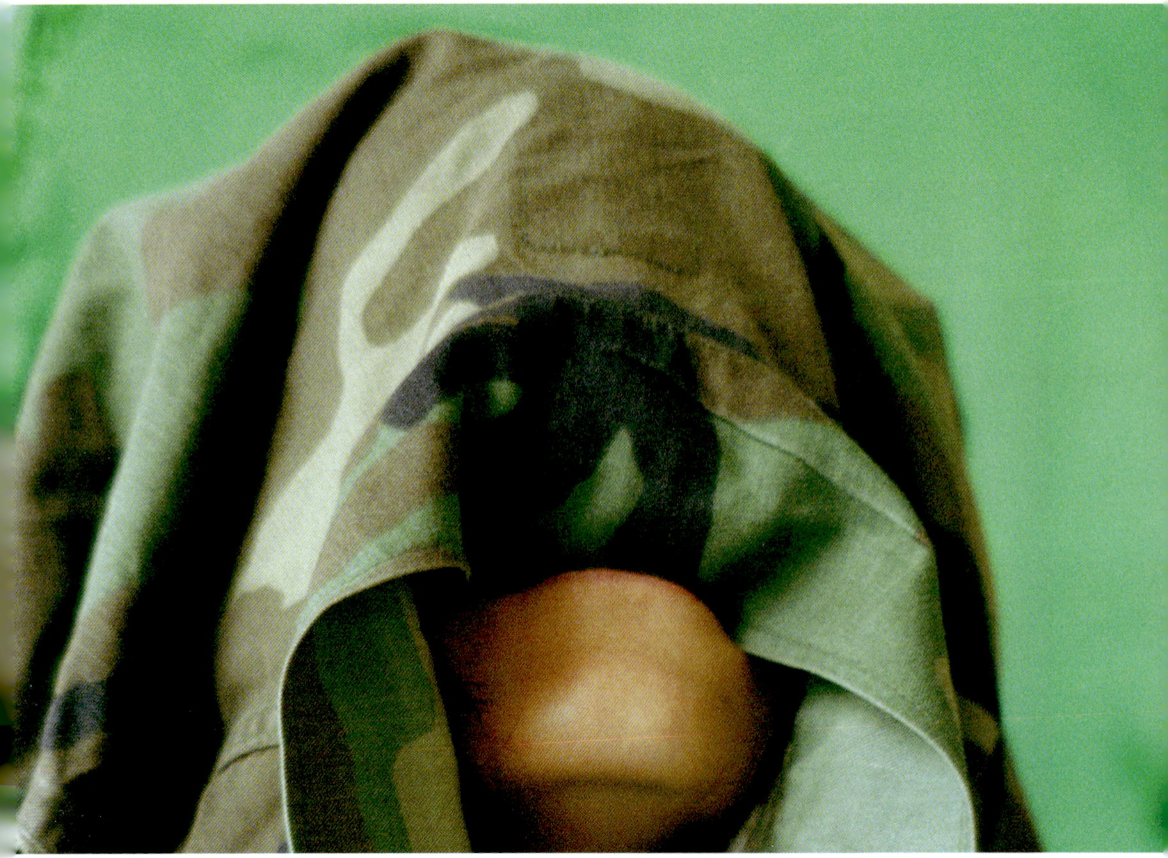

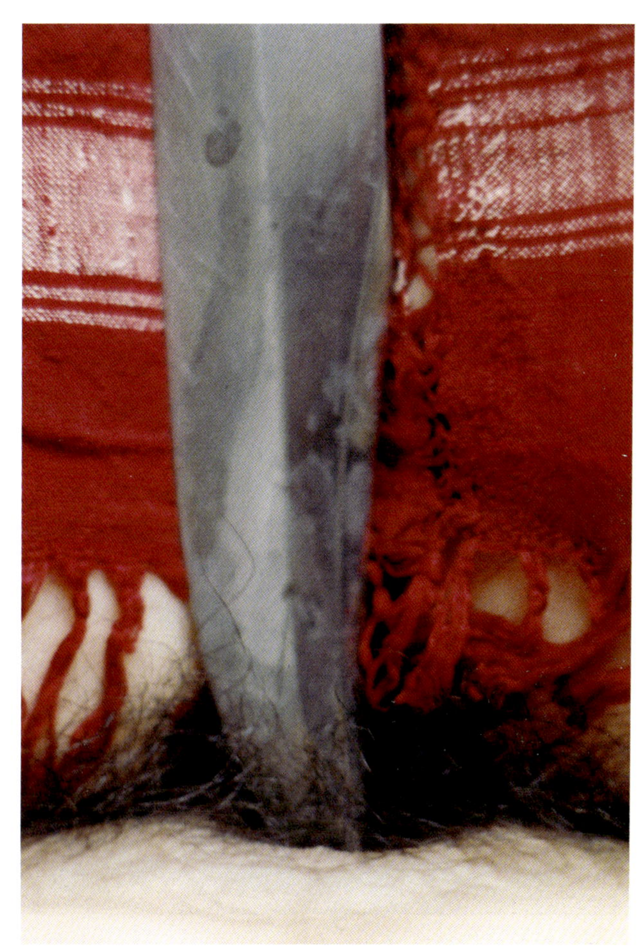

ausfinger. 2003

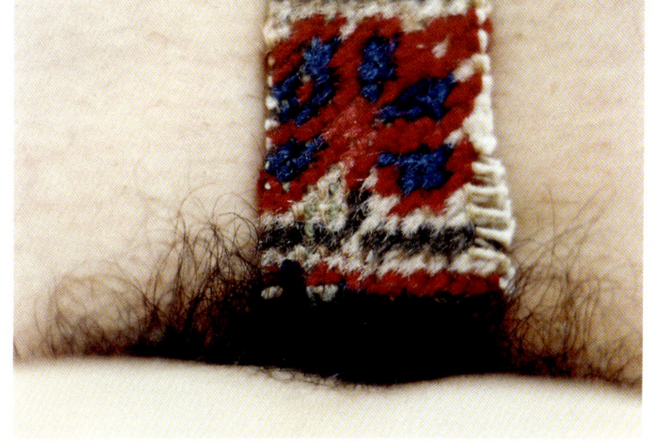

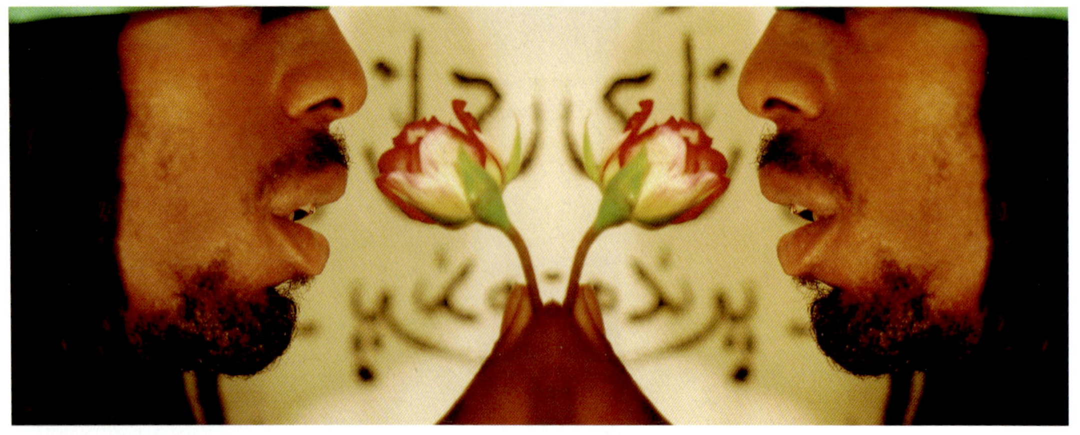

trust the garden, 2003

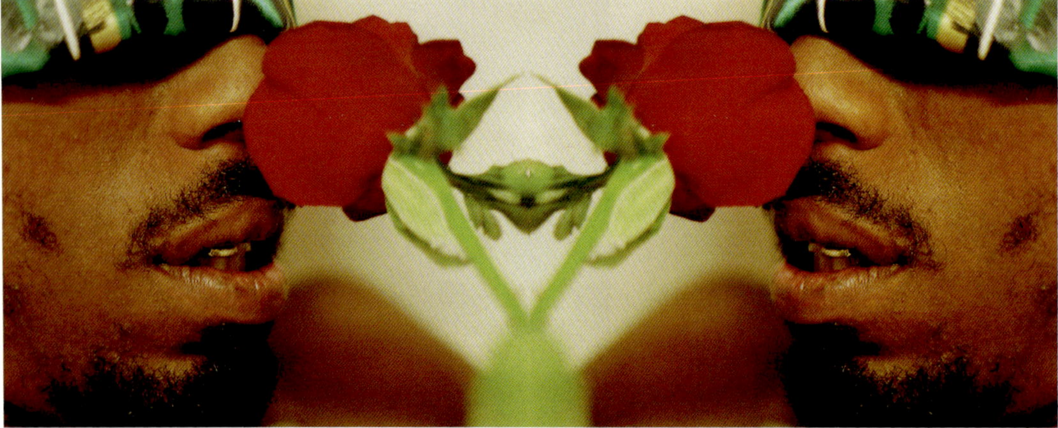

oh, 2019-20

JORDAN AMIRKHANI

Here and There, Textile and Exile: A Tangle as Framework

There is no sound, no articulation that is adequate to what injustice and power inflict . . . But there are approximations.[1]

In his 1984 text "Reflections on Exile," postcolonial theorist Edward Said described political displacement as an "unhealable rift forced between a human being and a native place, between the self and its true home."[2] Underscoring the dialectical relationship between identity and exile, Said's definition points to the traumatic rupture of living and being "out of place" as if it was akin to a tear or rip, splitting the very narrative of a life in two.

[1]   Edward Said, "From Silence to Sound and Back Again: Music, Literature, and History." *Raritan* 17, no. 2 (Fall 1997): 21.

[2]   Edward Said, "Reflections on Exile," *Granta* 13 (1984), reprinted in Russell Ferguson, Martha Gever, Trinh T. Min-ha, and Cornel West, eds., *Out There: Marginalization and Contemporary Cultures* (New York and Cambridge, MA: New Museum of Contemporary Art and MIT Press, 1990), 366.

Despite the proliferation of critical discourse in diaspora studies today, its primary concerns remain the "dis/re-location of peoples, the socio-cultural consequences, and conception of theoretical frameworks."[3] Rarely does the discourse seek to attend to the aesthetic or materialist parameters of exile—how it grows into (or out of) form, or bunches and gathers around a single life. But just as the body in exile travels across borders and territories, so too does the exiled artist's praxis as it struggles to affix itself in the frayed space between "there" and "here," "then" and "now." Artist Farkhondeh Shahroudi's works in textile gives form to the spaces within the fray, using historical, national, social, and personal constructions of fiber-based materials as surfaces upon which traces of the exilic experience—*her* exilic experience—bind and coil. Employing a strategy of un-settlement, Shahroudi's works make knots of the encounter between form and biography, and point to the discontinuous dynamics of exile and textile—turning a tangle into a framework.

[3]   Sieglinde Lemke, "Diaspora Aesthetics: Exploring the African Diaspora in the Works of Aaron Douglas, Jacob Lawrence, and Jean-Michel Basquiat," in *Exiles, Diasporas, and Strangers* (Cambridge, MA: MIT Press), 123.

Brimming with the intimacies of bodily experience, textiles are utilitarian objects laden with meaning. Decorating homes and religious spaces, covering bodies and beds, textiles are tactile communication tools, harboring memories and histories, traditions and tastes. Long associated with the gendered and racialized activities of the domestic and the decorative, textiles bear an embodied politics in spite of their marginalized status "within [European and American] museums and collections."[4] Thick and dense, it is no surprise that Roland Barthes seized upon fiber-based metaphors in his work on textual interpretation—a process that took seriously the etymological origins of text, textile, *techne* (craftsmanship), and *textere* (to weave), which he described as similar to unfurling threads from a knot.[5][6] From this position, the connection between tactility and speech, craft and translation, and the ways in which life is made meaningful through the transposition and unpicking of signs, looms large in my engagement with Shahroudi's textiles, most prominently in her works featuring Persian carpets.

[4]   Jenni Sorkin, "Affinities in Abstraction: Textiles, Otherness, and Painting in the 1970s," in the exhibition catalogue *Outliers and American Vanguard Art*, ed. Lynne Cooke (Chicago: University of Chicago Press, 2018), 93; and Julia Bryan-Wilson, "Introduction: Textile Politics," in *Fray: Art and Textile Politics* (Chicago: University of Chicago Press, 2017), 4-15.

[5]   Victoria Mitchell, "Textiles, Text and Techne" (1997), in *The Textile Reader*, 2nd edition, ed. Jessica Hemmings (London: Bloomsbury Publishing, 2023), 5-13; and Catherine Dormor, "Writing Textile, Making Text: Cloth and Stitch as Agency for Disorderly Text" (2014), in *Textile Society of America's Symposium Proceedings*, 2014. http://digitalcommons.unl.edu/tsaconf/926.

[6]   Roland Barthes, "Analyse textuelle d'un conte d'Edgar Poe," in *Semiotique narrative et textuelle*, ed. Claude Chabrol (Paris: Larousse, 1973), 29-54.

Shahroudi establishes the prominence of textiles early in her practice. Excited by Persian carpets as a young painting student at Al Zahra University in Tehran in the mid-1980s, their overt appearance begins in the midst of Shahroudi's coursework in textile design at Technical University-Dortmund—just a few years after Germany granted her political asylum.[7] Attuned to the long identification of handwoven carpetmaking in Iranian visual culture with spiritual perfection and utopian world-building, Shahroudi's engagement with the form exposes a desire to work with (and alongside) signifiers of home.[8]

[7]   Shahroudi was granted political asylum in Germany in 1990, leaving Iran in the long aftermath of the 1979 Revolution and in the midst of her political activism against government oppression and gender-based violence. See the Villa Romana's webpage for a brief biographical account of Shahroudi's career. https://www.villaromana.org/front_content.php?&idcat=278&changelang=3&idart=984.

[8]   Shahroudi's work in textiles and Persian carpets, specifically, has been contextualized by a powerful cohort of scholars working in Germany and Italy. Their attention to the artist's investments in the carpet's history and material reality was incredibly useful in my own research for this project. However, I felt that while there were many exegetical operations connecting Shahroudi's work to exile, there was less attention paid to how these formal and material operations manifested in the textiles themselves as well as in the affective nature of textile as a substance with its own objecthood and aesthetic properties. I hope my essay fills in some of this gap.

A selection of paintings from the late 1990s, such as *mobilergarten* (1999) show the artist working out a hybrid style of painting and textile, signaling a strategy of picture-making capable of holding two distinct genres and cultural traditions together. Shahroudi's effort to

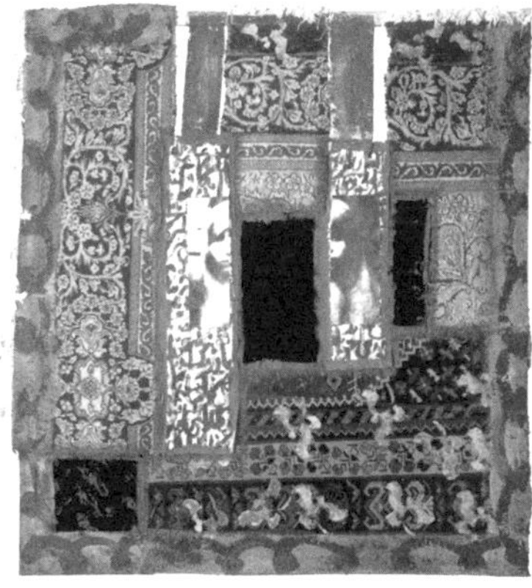

mobilergarten, 1999. Courtesy: the artist

communicate the control and choice at work in each form is intentional, allowing craft and painterly gesture to face off as equals, in open defiance of textile's presumed inferiority. However, the encounter is not seamless. The stressed surfaces of Shahroudi's canvases, many of them slashed and stitched with red thread, belie the struggle to hold the material to the picture's surface and the disjunctive qualities separating the capacious fluidity of paint from the bulky densities of the patterned carpet pieces. And yet, they bear each other, the real and the copy, bound to one another in rough juxtaposition, by force not choice.

It seems easy to interpret Shahroudi's exercise in hybridity as connected to her status as a new arrival to Europe—her struggles on the canvas perhaps mirroring struggles in the wider world. And yet, the artist's use of Persian carpets points to a freedom and transmutability of orientation and composition outside the purviews of European academic painting. Shahroudi explains:

> Carpets are not hierarchical, there is no up or down, you can turn them however you want and will still get the same form. I would do the same with my paintings and treat them as if they were carpets.[9]

This playful, non-distinction between painting and textile thrusts Shahroudi's painting practice into three-dimensional space like a Persian carpet spreading out, over, and into a room.[10]

[9]   Noushin Afzali, interview, "On Drawing and Language: The Work of Farkhondeh Shahroudi," *BERLINARTLINK: An Online Magazine for Contemporary Art*, December 16, 2022. https://wwwberlinartlink.com/2022/12/16/max-beckmann-war-nicht-hier-farkhondeh-shahroudi/.

[10]   This essay only attends to Shahroudi's three-dimensional work and will leave her performance practice to someone else.

Shahroudi's centering of carpet textiles begins in her series of installations known as the *gardens* or *mobile gardens*—a body of work using handwoven carpets, bought and found secondhand by the artist in stores across Germany. Whether stretched and layered on the floor, wrapped around the façade of a building, or pasted like a second skin onto the trunks and branches of trees, Shahroudi's carpets renegotiate the spatial relationship between an artwork and the environment that presents or supports it. For Shahroudi, a conception of cross-cultural spatiality and world-making is in play, most prominently in the artist's emphasis on the tradition of Safavid (Kerman) *chahar bagh* designs in Persian carpets, which feature a four-quadrant rectilinear garden surrounded by walls—a plan unique to the Islamic world, and an early iteration of "paradise" on Earth.[11] An exercise in visual balance, traditional *chahar bagh* carpets brim with rhythmic patterns and sinuous stylizations and seek to hold the tastes and interests of the atelier and patron in harmony with a shared set of symbolic features. Almost all include a singular

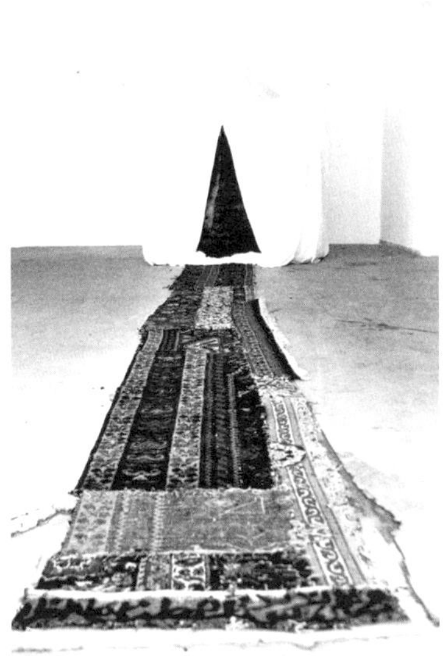
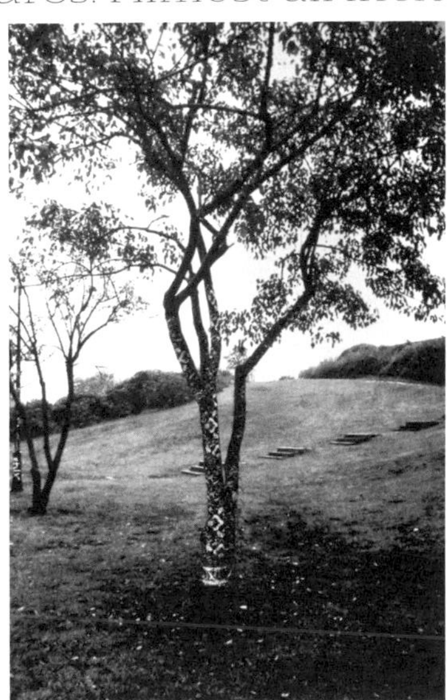

mobile garden, 2000, *Continental Shift* installation view at Stadsgalerij Heerlen, 2000. Courtesy: the artist.
garden in the garden/madjnoun, 2003. Courtesy: the artist.

fountain and a path of geometric water channels that intersect the plane-like avenues, their borders planted with rows of trees, shrubs, flowers in bloom, ripened fruit, and creatures symbolic of spiritual perfection and beauty such as peacocks, songbirds, waterfowl, goldfish, and gazelles. A world, laid flat, placed elsewhere, Shahroudi presses against the European reduction of Islamic art to mere ornament, instantiating the conceptual and political origins of the carpet's abstraction and its portable nature. This is certainly true of her 2003 work *giardino*, in which Sharoudi assembles a long floor runner composed of strips and squares of carpets, the parts sewn and rearranged into a new composition. A model of harmony between natural and human life, the *chahar bagh* presents a "utopian" vision of the world predicated on the body's alignment with/in it—an ideal Shahroudi interrupts and reorders into a new geographical arrangement, transforming and renegotiating her world according to her own needs and desires.

[11]   Mohammad Gharipour, *Persian Gardens and Pavilions: Reflections in History* (London: I.B. Tauris, 2013). In Farsi, *chahar bagh* means "four gardens," and is a Persian and Indo-Persian quadrilateral garden that originated in the paradise gardens of the Achaemenid Empire, as suggested by excavations of Pasagardae and Susa in the early twentieth-century.

Whether Shahroudi's "mobile gardens" celebrate or critique the notion of utopia on earth remains in question. Titled in reference to Michel Foucault's 1967

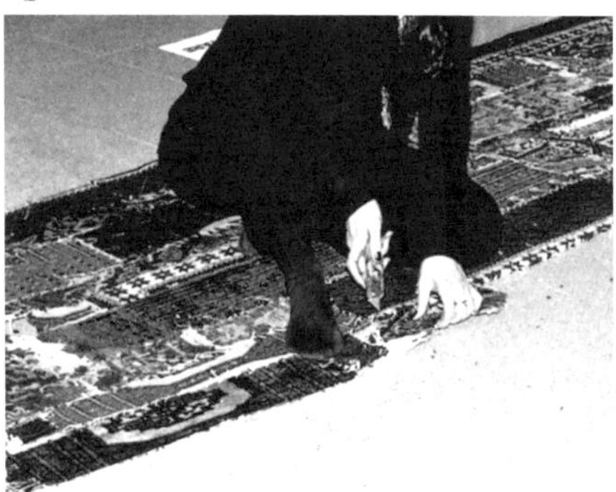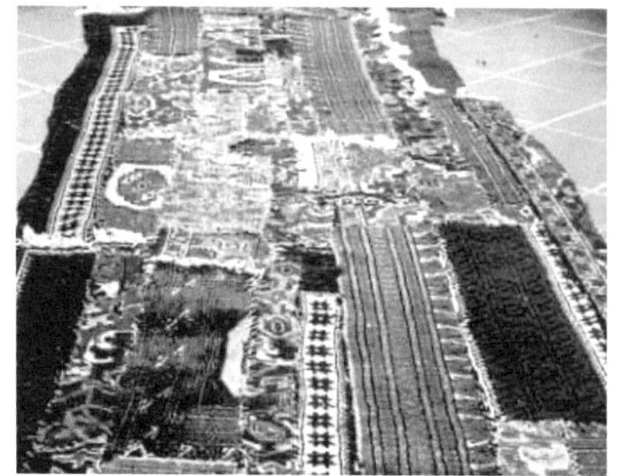

giardino (details), 2003, performance at Stazione Tiburtina, Rome, 2003. Coutesy: the artist.

lecture, "Des Spaces Autres" in which he defines "heterotopic spaces" across histories and geographies—spaces that exist in reality, but remain separate from it, such as the cinema, libraries, museums, and for Foucault, the Persian garden and its representation in carpets—Shahroudi's "gardens" collapse and confuse spatial territories, renegotiating what is inside and outside, and therefore, where an object "belongs."[12] In Shahroudi's *garten/bagh* (2004), an installation composed of eleven handmade carpets sited on the grounds of the Haus der Kulturen der Welt in Berlin, carpets move from the private, interior sphere to the public outdoors. Wrapped tightly around the branches of trees or the exterior of architectural supports, the installations present as bandage or skin, stuck seamlessly to their surfaces. The textile's bright colorations and thick patterning stutter against the minimal institutionalism of Germany public space, enacting the tension of difference and assimilation at once. Again, this juxtaposition invokes a politics of the migrant, seeking new space outside one's home, and perhaps the condition of the refugee, whose place in the world has been thrust into uncertainty. That the field of the textile, which in some cases provides cover or comfort, relief or nostalgia, lives in tandem with its visible difference, is part of Shahroudi's emphasis. Just as

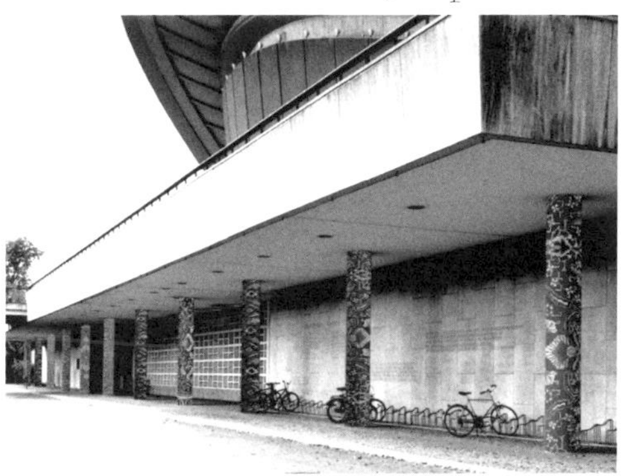

garten/bagh, 2004, *Far Near Distance—New Positions of Iranian Artists* installation view at Haus der Kulturen der Welt, Berlin, 2004. Courtesy: the artist

utopias are always-already a fantasy, so too is the immigrant's fantasy of perfect accommodation. Her carpet installations claim a space for herself and others like her, proclaiming themselves "here."

[12] Michel Foucault, "Des Espaces Autres" (1967), in *Architecture/Mouvement/Continuité*, trans. Jay Miskowiec (October 1984): 1-9.

Shahroudi's series of floor sculptures, known as *seed bombs* (2017-ongoing) or "flying carpets" leverage the artist's engagement with carpet materiality into new formal, linguistic, and political constellations. No longer seamless with their environs, these works are studies in swaddling, squeezing, and bunching, their shape determined by the fingers of black ties (stretched out bicycle tubing) that strangle the thick material into shape.[13] Arranged in small groups of two or three, these ambiguous bundles hold a latent pressure, their titles invoking immanent violence or faulty weaponry, an explosion of regenerative growth or an act of terror. Marking the entwined collapse of political and economic relations between Iran and Western powers since the 1979 Revolution, the rise of theocratic rule and gender apartheid under Khomeini's government, the destructive consequences catalyzed by the War on Terror, and onwards towards the recent visa and travel bans imposed by Donald Trump, the escalation of military

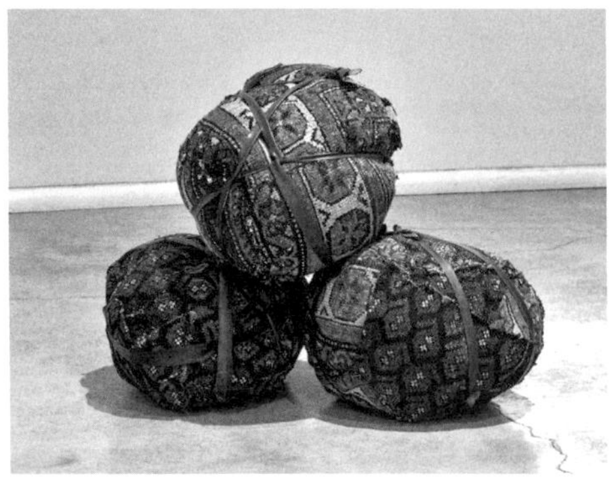

seed bombs, 2024, *Farkhondeh Shahroudi: of weeping trees* installation view at Goethe-Institut New York, 2024. Photo: Marc Tatti

operations by proxy Iranian militias across the Middle East, and the subsequent destabilization of the region, the greatest victims of these historical failures remain the Iranian people who endure or escape, emigrate or self-destruct. In this way, they share the bombastic trajectories of all displaced people, thrust by force into new rooms, their surfaces bent by the impact, strangled by institutional bureaucracy, and marked as potentially dangerous, their lives full of tangles.

[13]   Dr. Alma-Elisa Kittner, "blossoming. Farkhondeh Shahroudi's spatial poetry and poetic-political spaces," in the exhibition catalogue *Wir sind die Feder in des Schreibers Hand, wohin wir gehen, is tuns nicht bekannt* (Berlin: Staatliche Museen zu Berlin, 2023), 30–50.

> *ghah ghah (ha ha)*, 2020. Courtesy: the artist
> *ambulance virtual leg*, 2006-10, *force times distance: on labour and its sonic ecologies* installation view at sonsbeek20–24 international contemporary art exhibition, Arnhem, 2021. Photo: Django van Ardenne
> Farkhondeh Shahroudi's studio, Berlin, 2022. Courtesy: the artist

> *oh*, 2021; *seed bomb*, 2021; *antiflag (anna mermaid)*, 2021/*performative poetics of matter*, 2021, *force times distance: on labour and its sonic ecologies* installation view at sonsbeek20–24 international contemporary art exhibition, Arnhem, 2021. Photo: Django van Ardenne
> *seed bomb*, 2021; *antiflag (anna mermaid)*, 2021/ *performative poetics of matter*, 2021, *force times distance: on labour and its sonic ecologies* installation view at sonsbeek20–24 international contemporary art exhibition, Arnhem, 2021. Photo: Django van Ardenne

> *book in the book*, 2001-ongoing. Courtesy: the artist

> *mime - epitome present*, 2006. Courtesy: the artist

> *antiflag (of weeping trees)*, 2024, *Farkhondeh Shahroudi: of weeping trees* installation view at Goethe-Institut New York, 2024. Photo: Marc Tatti
> *antiflag (sky is no ones ground)*, 2019, performance at Exile Visual Arts Award, Berlin, 2023. Photo: Till Budde
> *antiflag (hair demonstration)*, 2017, performance at Lottozero, Prato, 2017. Photo: Francesco Gnot

> *meine blumen sind nicht eure blumen?* (my flower is not your flower?), 2018, *WHOSE LAND HAVE I LIT ON NOW?, INVOCATION II* performance at SAVVY Contemporary, Berlin, 2018. Photo: Marvin Systermans

> *ausfinger* (from finger), 2003. Courtesy: the artist

> *ausfinger* (from finger), 2003. Courtesy: the artist

> *trust the garden*, 2003. Courtesy: the artist

> *unbounded books*, 2024/*unbounded books*, 2016-ongoing. Courtesy: the artist
> *oh*, 2019-20. Courtesy: the artist

For all full-bleed images: *Farkhondeh Shahroudi: of weeping trees* installation view at Goethe-Institut New York, 2024. Photo: Marc Tatti

FARKHONDEH SHAHROUDI (b. 1962, Tehran, Iran)
has been living and working in Berlin since 2001. Shahroudi studied painting at the Alzahra
University in Tehran until she was forced to seek political asylum in Germany in 1990, where she
continued her studies in Art and Design at Dortmund University. Her work has been exhibited
and housed at numerous galleries and museums, including Haus der Kulturen der Welt (HKW),
Berlin; SAVVY Contemporary - The Laboratory of Form-Ideas, Berlin; The British Museum, London;
and the Vehbi Koç Contemporary Art Foundation, Istanbul. She was the recipient of the 2017
Villa Romana Prize, the 2022 Hannah Höch Förderpreis, and the inaugural Exile Visual Arts
Award for 2024, among other distinctions.

ZACHARY B. FELDMAN, PH.D.
is curator of Visual Arts and Programs at the Goethe-Institut New York. He holds a joint-Ph.D.
in Comparative Media and German Studies from Vanderbilt University, and was a Helena
Rubenstein Fellow in Curatorial Studies at the Whitney Independent Study Program from
2022-23, where he co-curated *Clocking Out: Time Beyond Management* at Artists Space. Feldman's
exhibitions have been reviewed in the New York Times, and he has held previous curatorial
roles at the Frist Art Museum, Nashville, TN; Zentrum fur Kunst und Medien, Karlsruhe, and the
National Gallery of Art, Washington, DC.; and has guest curated for *e-flux Film*.

BILLY FOWO
is a curator and writer based in Berlin and working at SAVVY Contemporary - The Laboratory
of Form-Ideas. With points of interest in various fields and disciplines such as the sonic, linguis-
tics, and literature, Fowo questions what is considered to be knowledge and endeavors to rethink
the spaces in which it is disseminated. He recently graduated from de Appel's Curatorial
Programme 2023 and acted between 2021 and 2023 as a Tutor at the Dutch Art Institute (DAI),
in the framework of their COOP Academy.

JORDAN AMIRKHANI, PH.D.
is curator and Head of Research and Project Development at Rivers Institute for Contemporary
Art & Thought—a non-profit organization based in New Orleans, Louisiana committed to research
and publishing, exhibitions and convenings on art of the global diaspora. Prior to taking on
these roles, Amirkhani held academic positions at American University in Washington, DC and
the University of Tennessee in Chattanooga. Amirkhani's writing has been featured in many
national and international publications, including: *The Paris Review, Artforum, Art in America,
Baltimore Arts, Boston Art Review, X-Tra*, and *Burnaway.org*. Her emphasis on contextualizing
contemporary art and artists working in the American South garnered her a prestigious
Creative Capital/Andy Warhol Foundation "Short-Form" Writing Grant in 2017 and three nomi-
nations for The Rabkin Prize in Arts Journalism in 2017, 2018, and 2019.

This book is published on the occasion of the exhibition *Farkhondeh Shahroudi: of weeping trees* at the Goethe-Institut New York, May 16 - July 19, 2024, curated by Zachary B. Feldman.

EDITOR
Zachary B. Feldman

PUBLISHING EDITOR
Ilaria Bombelli

GRAPHIC DESIGN
Anna Azzali

COPYEDITING
Giulia Celuppi

FIRST EDITION 2024

Printed in Italy by Grafiche Antiga

ISBN 978-88-6749-653-2

€ 25 / $ 30

EDITED FOR
Goethe-Institut New York
30 Irving Place
New York, NY 10003
www.goethe.de/ins/us/en/sta/ney.html

PUBLISHED AND DISTRIBUTED BY
Mousse Publishing
Contrappunto s.r.l.
Via Pier Candido Decembrio 28,
20137, Milan-Italy

AVAILABLE THROUGH
Mousse Publishing, Milan
moussemagazine.it

ALL WORKS BY FARKHONDEH SHAHROUDI
© Farkhondeh Shahroudi

ALL RIGHTS RESERVED BY AUTHORS
© Jordan Amirkhani, Zachary B. Feldman,
Billy Fowo

© 2024 Mousse Publishing, Goethe-Institut
New York, the artist, the authors of the texts

ACKNOWLEDGEMENT
It takes a village to make an exhibition, and a book. There are so many people to thank, but first and foremost, I'd like to thank Farkhondeh Shahroudi, and her family and friends. It has been my absolute pleasure to get to know you here in New York. I'd also like to thank the Goethe-Institut, particularly the New York director, Jörg Schumacher, and the director of the Bildene Kunst Bereich in Munich, Eva Schmitt. Thank you for trusting the process. Next, I extend my gratitude to our interns, Alia Rosa Lübben, Olivia Al-Slaiman, and Nelya Rosa Ahmia, for your help at the various stages of the exhibition and book. Our A-Team, Mike Sanabria, Lee Grice, and Marc Paradise have always been ready to solve any problem during install–there's probably something in the basement that can help. Thanks also to Christian Amaya Garcia for your calming presence and ingenuity during a hectic install. A huge thank you goes out to Madelena Caron for copy and line editing contributions–I wish you the best of luck on your new journey. Thanks to Marc Tatti for the exhibition documentation, to Géza Schenk for the exhibition communication design, and to Ilaria Bombelli and Anna Azzali at Mousse for facilitating this publication. (Zachary B. Feldman)

Generous support for the exhibition *Farkhondeh Shahroudi: of weeping trees* and this publication is provided by the Körber Stiftung, the International Studio and Curatorial Program (ISCP), and Norse Airlines.

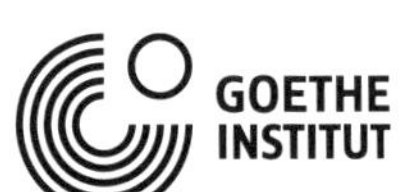
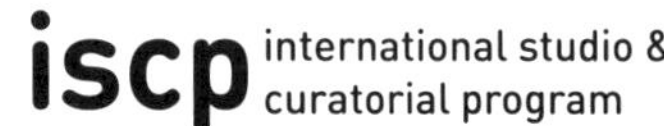
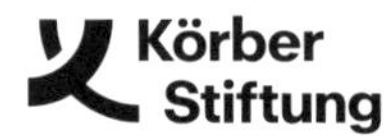
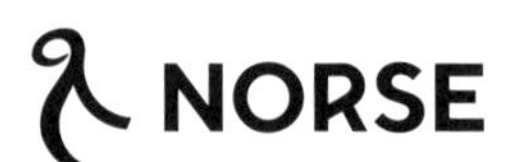